money with only cold, calculated rationale just doesn't work. How we connect to it on an emotional level helps shift daily or monthly routines, which can make all the difference. Stick with the little things, and you'll start to see how those huge, impossible-to-reach milestones feel much more achievable.

It really does start with a conversation, with shared experiences, and a willingness to find what works for you. So, if you feel more hopeful and confident about money on the other side of this book, we'll have done what we set out to do.

CW01499818

The information in this book on things like tax limits and government regulation was accurate in February 2025. You'll hear us say it a lot throughout, but always check the government website in case something's changed. While there are lots of useful tools in this book no matter where you live, it'll be most helpful to readers based in the UK. Finally, everyone's individual circumstances are unique, so this book won't give you financial or tax advice. Always do your own research and speak to a financial adviser before making decisions.

the book of money

Monzo is one of the UK's biggest banks, trusted by more than 12 million customers and counting. Founded in 2015, we're a digital bank that's revolutionised the industry and made millions of people feel better about their money. With smart tools and innovative features, we help customers grow more capable and confident in their finances than ever before.

Monzo will be donating the full share of their royalties, which is a minimum of £0.49 for each book sold in the UK, to a registered charity called Money Ready (charity number 1123791). They're dedicated to creating a financially fluent population by delivering education programmes to over 50,000 people across the UK every year. Money Ready works to help everyone feel more confident about their money by understanding it better – no matter what their starting point is. Find out more at www.moneyready.org.

the book of money

monzo

PENGUIN BOOKS

PENGUIN BOOKS

UK | USA | Canada | Ireland | Australia
India | New Zealand | South Africa

Penguin Books is part of the Penguin Random House group of companies
whose addresses can be found at global.penguinrandomhouse.com

Penguin Random House UK,
One Embassy Gardens, 8 Viaduct Gardens, London SW11 7BW

penguin.co.uk

First published 2025
001

Copyright © Monzo Bank Limited, 2025

Set in 10.2/15.6pt Aestetico
Typeset by Six Red Marbles UK, Thetford, Norfolk

Printed and bound in Great Britain by Clays Ltd, Elcograf S.p.A.

The authorised representative in the EEA is Penguin Random House Ireland,
Morrison Chambers, 32 Nassau Street, Dublin D02 YH68

A CIP catalogue record for this book is available from the British Library

ISBN: 978–1–804–94866–8

Penguin Random House is committed to a sustainable future
for our business, our readers and our planet. This book is made
from Forest Stewardship Council® certified paper.

Contents

Foreword by TS Anil, CEO of Monzo

This is a book about money. Not the history of money, or money as some abstract concept, but money as it exists in your life. How you spend it, what it means you can do in the future and, most importantly, how it makes you feel.

I grew up in India, in a home where we had many things to be grateful for, but little money. I went on to become an always broke college student, and it wasn't until I started working in finance that I really thought about my own relationship with money.

Like me, you might have learned how to calculate the length of a hypotenuse in maths classes at school. But chances are, you were expected to figure out what a mortgage is on your own, as an adult. That's because a formal financial education isn't common. In fact, it's exceptional. It can seem like some people just 'get' money, magically, overnight. Then the world is suddenly divided into those who are 'money people' and those who aren't. If you fall into the second camp, you might be afraid to ask questions in case you sound stupid, and you're not the only one.

I've been lucky enough to live and work in countries all over the world, each with their own set of attitudes and traditions connected to money. But one thing they all have in common? When money talk is on the table, people freeze up. This reluctance to be open and honest leaves valid questions unanswered, and shared experiences unheard.

Although money is one of very few universal human experiences, it often makes people feel awkward, anxious and uncomfortable. Just plain bad. So bad that a third of 18- to 44-year-olds say they'd rather scrub a toilet than check their savings account.[1] That's not surprising – over the last few years, we've experienced major economic crises, regional wars and a global pandemic. We've grown accustomed to a financial industry designed to catch people out, not build them up. And the milestones of previous generations seem unattainable to younger people, so trying can feel pointless. It's no wonder money anxiety is a real and growing issue that hits millennials and Gen Z the hardest.

If any (or most) of this is resonating with you, you're not alone. We know that because we're a bank that speaks to millions of customers who feel the same way. And we've seen how, despite the difficult realities, small changes can have a hugely positive impact on people's relationship with their finances.

There's proof of that in each chapter in this book. We'll share stories inspired by our customers' real-life experiences of money, and the tools, habits and changes that transformed their financial lives. All while acknowledging that approaching

Part 1

Would you rather look at your bank balance or your reflection when you've just woken up?

Chapter 1
Looking in the money mirror

Let's start with a confession: this book doesn't know you personally. Unless you're Greg from our office. *Greg, we're always watching.*

When it comes to your relationship with money, you're in charge. That's why it's important to figure out how *you* feel about it. Your feelings might seem random, but they all come from somewhere. Maybe you hate woolly sweaters because you had to wear one every Christmas, or love meal deals because they remind you of your student days. Sometimes, the reason is obvious. Other times, we have no idea why we love or hate the things we do. You might be obsessed with tarantulas, or terrified of ice cream, and never feel the need to ask yourself *why*. The truth is, how we feel about money doesn't come from what we've read in a textbook. Instead, we pick things up from those around us. Four out of five people say they learned about money from their parents,[1] but that could mean anything from *'my mum is an accountant'* to *'my dad ate pennies as a party trick'*.

The world of finance hasn't always made it easy to understand what's going on. It's filled with jargon, complicated maths, and people who seem like they were born wearing a suit and tie. But it doesn't have to be like that. If you use money, then you can understand it – you just need to find a way that works for you.

Money and me

Sure, how you manage your money is personal, but there's also so much you can't control. Over the last few years we've lived through a perfect storm: low wage growth, skyrocketing energy and food bills, and childcare costs that could be a downpayment on a private jet. A tough economy only deepens inequalities that already exist – like race, gender and generational wealth – which help some people and hurt others. These are problems that no one can life-hack their way out of, and we won't pretend that's the case. They only make it even more important to focus on the things you *can* control and change. And if thinking about the economy and your entire origin story feels like a lot, we have good news. You don't have to think about that all at once – in fact, you actively shouldn't. Because if you thought about those things constantly, nothing would get done, and your head would possibly explode. It's about focusing on what you really want, a little at a time.

The hardest part is starting. But once you do, it feels a lot more doable, which makes you feel a whole lot better.

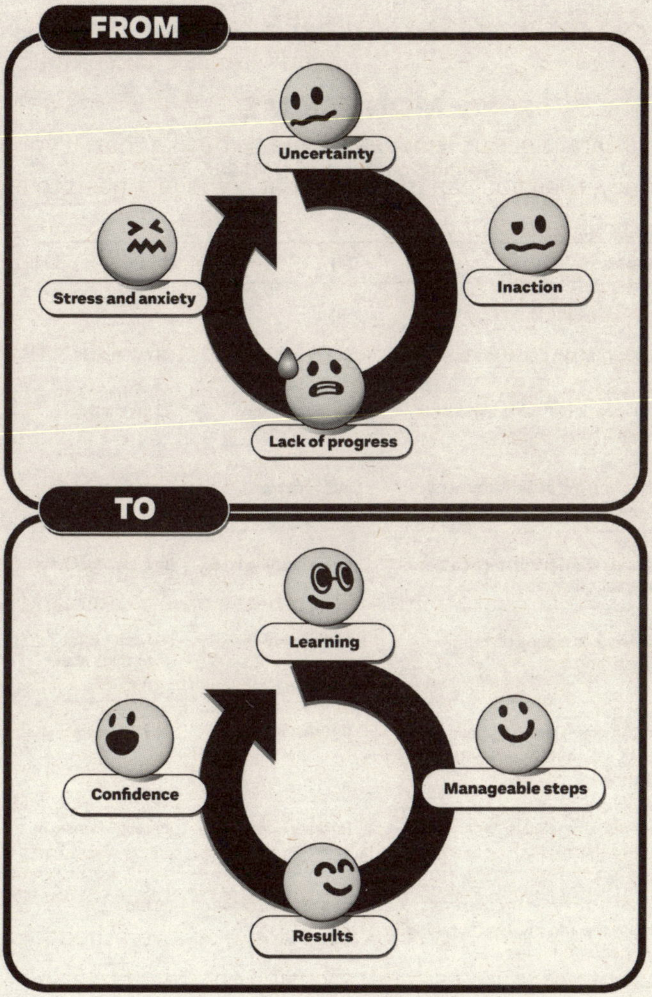

FROM

Uncertainty

Stress and anxiety

Inaction

Lack of progress

TO

Learning

Confidence

Manageable steps

Results

So let's hold up the money mirror. What's going on in your brain when it comes to your finances? What's working? What's not? What do you want to change? Yep, it's time for a quiz . . .

MONEY & ME

1507 Prosperity Lane,
Sterling-on-Thames, MM1 9RR,
United Kingdom

Question	(a)	(b)
I usually make decisions based on...	(a) my budget	(b) my mood
The idea of following a monthly budget feels...	(a) reassuring	(b) restrictive
Checking my bank statement makes me feel...	(a) in control	(b) stressed out
Changing my bank to get a better interest rate sounds like...	(a) something I'd do	(b) a lot of effort
Paying into a pension is something...	(a) I already do	(b) I don't want to think about just yet
Tracking and splitting holiday costs with another person makes me feel...	(a) fine	(b) a little worried
A serious-looking letter arrives from my bank. I...	(a) open it straight away	(b) delay opening it
Putting myself in my overdraft to buy me and my dog matching jumpers sounds like...	(a) a terrible idea	(b) fun

RECEIPT 20150202

If you answered mostly a), you tend to make money decisions based on facts, not feelings. You probably have a budget, a plan and a back-up plan for the back-up plan. You're on the right track, but don't forget, it's OK to treat yourself now and then.

If you answered mostly b), you go with your gut and live for quick wins. When things are working out, this feels great, but it can mean you're not thinking ahead. Luckily, a bit of planning can make those splurges feel less risky.

If you answered a mix of the two, you might change your approach based on what's going on in your life. Or perhaps you're pretty confident with some aspects of money, like your monthly budget, but less sure about others, like interest rates.

Whatever you answered, take a moment to notice what emotions popped up. Did you feel stressed? Anxious? Hungry? Take a deep breath and make yourself a snack, because wherever you're starting from, we've got your back.

Goals and me

In the simplest terms, a financial goal is an objective that you set for your money. It's worth reflecting on what yours might be before you dive into the rest of this book. A money goal can be for the short, medium or long term, and having one can help you focus on what really matters.

As our lives change – from leaving home, to having kids, and finally owning a full set of Volcanic Orange Le Creuset cookware – our goals will likely change, too. Broadly, we understand your financial life as having three stages. Transitioning from one stage to another can take years, and where you're at isn't necessarily linked to your age. Setbacks are normal, progress isn't linear, and you might find you don't fit perfectly into one stage. Perhaps you're starting afresh in your 50s after a divorce, or getting a boost in your 20s when your side hustle takes off. Think less age brackets, more Taylor Swift 'Eras'.

Era One:
Starting out or starting over

Era Two:
Planning ahead

Era Three:
Comfort building

Era One: starting out or starting over

Whether you're moving out of your family home, or recovering from a setback later in life, the goal is simple: survive. You're living pay cheque to pay cheque, covering rent and bills, and maybe even saving a little bit for something fun.

Your goals in this era might include:
- Covering daily expenses
- Learning how to budget
- Setting money aside for fun, like nights out and gigs
- Paying off student loans or credit card debt
- Building a *safety net* – your emergency fund for unexpected costs
- Saving for something small but meaningful
- Earning a steady income

Era Two: planning ahead

Now you're juggling. You've got more than just survival on your mind – you're trying to save for the bigger stuff while keeping the lights on. Maybe you've started thinking more about your future; saving up for a home deposit or putting more into your pension. You might be sharing finances with a partner, or taking on responsibility for kids or dogs (dogs are expensive).

Your goals now involve thinking both short term and long term:

- Splurging on fancier treats
- Starting to support or look after others, like kids or ageing relatives
- Setting aside some fun money for holidays or social events
- Contributing regularly to your pension
- Paying off significant debts, like a car loan
- Preparing for career pivots or new side hustles
- Saving for a house deposit or a bigger place

Era Three: comfort building

You're in a stronger position career-wise and financially, and you're thinking more about the long game. You're focused on thriving, not just surviving.

Your goals in this era might be:
- Paying off your mortgage
- Budgeting for bigger and better experiences
- Investing
- Reviewing your current pension plan or planning for retirement
- Saving for your kids' future, or supporting ageing relatives
- Organising your will (sorting out what happens to your things when you're gone)

Wherever you are, it's easy to get caught up in what life *should* look like by now, because of family, friends, or perfectly filtered social media feeds. Try not to compare. Just because your friend has a shiny new car, a six-word job title, or a massive Pokémon card collection, it doesn't mean you're falling behind. Progress rarely moves in a straight line, and that's OK. The aim isn't perfection, or becoming a briefcase-toting 'money person' who gets giddy over colour-coded expense charts. It's all about finding what works for you.

We're not going to give you advice or tell you exactly what to do. (Unless you're Greg. *Don't buy that shirt, Greg. It doesn't suit you*.) But that won't stop us from breaking down the basics, sharing stories inspired by our customers, and exploring tried-and-tested strategies that'll help you feel more confident and capable than ever. We'll start with the fundamentals of personal finance, like budgeting, sharing helpful hacks that have worked for literally millions of others. Then we'll tackle the most complex topics in the simplest terms – think debt, investments, retirement and anything else that makes you want to run for the hills.

Read it in one go or dip in whenever you need to – you're in charge!

Chapter 2
Principles for your money

With the introductions done, it's time to get started. These principles are the seven key themes that will guide your financial journey. We found them carved into gold tablets deep inside an ancient cave . . . Well actually, they're real methods tried and trusted by our Monzo community – real people, just like you, who've found what works for them. No archaeological expedition necessary.

You'll see these principles pop up in every chapter. Let's break them down so you can hit the ground running.

1. Use time to your advantage
All good books need a hero and a villain. When it comes to the story of your money, think of *compounding* as the hero, and *inflation* as the villain. Once you understand how those two things can work for or against your money over time, everything else follows!

COMPOUND INTEREST CAFE

28 Savings Street,
Manchester, M15 4QD,
United Kingdom

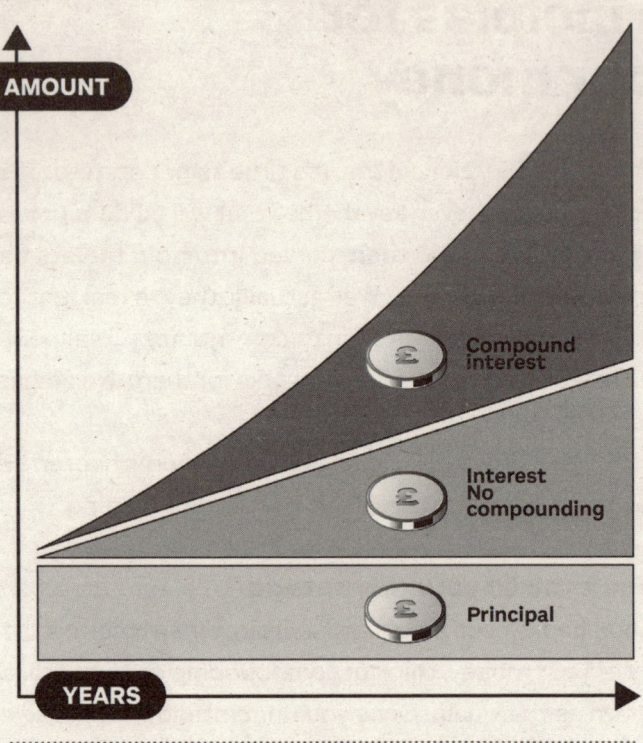

Thank you! Come again!

The hero: compound interest and returns

The villain: inflation

Einstein called compound interest the eighth wonder of the world, with good reason. When you leave your money to grow over time and don't touch your savings, compounding is the interest you earn on your interest. Think of it as the financial version of 'that escalated quickly'. It turns your money into a snowball that gets bigger as it rolls downhill. When you're saving for the future over a long period of time, this changes everything.

And when you invest your money, you're doing so in the hope you'll benefit from compound returns. That's when an investment does well and you reinvest what you've gained from it, to keep your money growing.

If compounding is your money's best friend, then inflation is its enemy. Inflation is the rate at which things increase in price over time. It's why you can buy less with the same amount of money today compared to five years ago.

That means if you let your money sit in an account that doesn't earn any interest over the years, it's slowly going to be worth less over time.

Patience over long periods of time is a superpower when it comes to managing your money. That's because the longer you give your money to work for you, the bigger the rewards, all thanks to the power of compounding.

We'll dig into compound interest, returns and inflation in lots more detail in the savings and investments chapters.

2. Pay yourself first

'Pay yourself first' is the short way of saying: when payday hits, squirrel away some money into your debt repayments, savings and investments before you buy anything. This should be the first thing we do, but more often than not, we only save what we have left. Instead, you should think of your savings as a salary that you pay to your future self.

Think about the joy of finding a tenner stuffed in a pocket of a jacket you haven't worn in ages. That's what paying yourself first feels like – a gift from your past self to your future self.

Sure, your present self might want to swipe that cash and spend it, but if you put in enough systems and reminders to stop this from happening, your future self will thank you.

Starting with even the smallest amount can make a big difference. It will add up. It will help cushion you in an emergency. And most importantly, it will build a habit. Make this task even easier by automating your savings – set it up once, and you won't have to think about it.

3. Make your goals personal

This book will talk a lot about the *hows* of managing money, but you'll need to find your own personal *whys* to stay motivated. These *whys* will be the driving force behind every financial decision you make. Maybe you dream about going on a luxury trip, moving to a brand new city, or simply building up a

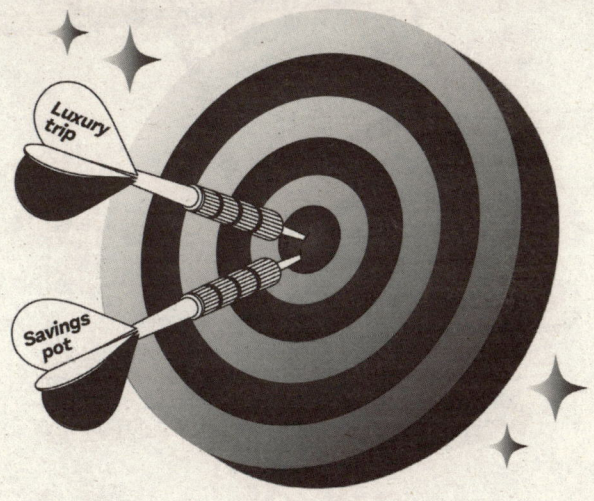

savings pot. Whatever it is, having a goal will give your money intention and help you focus on the things that really matter to you. And did you know, writing your goals down (or finding pictures that represent them) can make a huge difference to whether or not you'll actually achieve them.[1] Neuroscience shows that when you write down your goals, you're using both the logical and creative parts of your brain, which boosts your chances of success.[2] Plus, getting them down on paper makes them real and tangible, helping you prioritise them.

4. Embrace the envelope method

The envelope method is an old-school way to manage your money, but like quality denim or your nana's dating advice, it still holds up. You label envelopes with categories like rent, food and entertainment, and then stash the cash you've budgeted for each inside. Once the envelope's empty, that's it – no more spending on that category. Today, you can do this digitally using banking apps, by allocating your income to different 'pots'. The idea is exactly the same: give every pound a job and keep an eye on where it's going. Just don't forget to include an envelope for paying yourself first! We'll cover this in detail in the 'Balancing your budget' chapter.

5. Future-proof your income

Generally speaking, you'll have money coming in – your income – and money going out – your expenses. Over time, you'll also want to keep some of that money aside for savings and investments. That third category might not always be a priority, like when you're younger or if you're focusing on repaying debts, and that's OK. You just want to get in the habit of building it up over time, because it'll help you create financial security for the future. You can boost how much you put into it by spending less, earning more, or both! Your income might increase if you get a pay rise, pick up a side hustle as a Vinted mogul, or claim all the benefits you're entitled to. Your expenses might decrease if you curb a coffee habit or a child moves out. Building the percentage that goes in that third pot over time really does add up (thanks to that sweet, sweet compound interest).

Think of it this way: if you spend £4.50 on a coffee, once you drink it, it's gone – no lasting impact. But if you use that £4.50 to plant a coffee bean, you'll get a coffee plant, and over time that plant can produce enough beans to make *many* cups of coffee. It's like 'teach a man to fish' but you're way more caffeinated. Increasing how much you invest and save of your income is like growing the plant – it can provide you with more value in the future, helping you build wealth rather than living pay cheque to pay cheque.

6. Don't compare yourself to others

It's totally normal to notice what your friends are spending their money on, but things get tricky when you start measuring your own success against their purchases. Whether it's upmarket restaurants, a new car, or a flat with a south-facing balcony, comparing yourself to others can send you spiralling into self-doubt and impulse buys.

The truth is that everyone's money situation is different and, more importantly, you'll never get the full story. Some friends might seem to have endless cash but could be racking up debt. Others might appear to have effortlessly saved for a house deposit but were actually gifted money by their parents. Instead of trying to match what they have or feeling guilty about what you don't, it's important to stay grounded in your own financial realities and goals. So stick to your own values, know your limits, and steer clear of the comparison game. Which brings us to . . .

7. Celebrate your wins

Every time you reach a money milestone, take a moment to celebrate. Whether you've paid off a credit card, saved your first £1,000, or added a bit extra to your pension, these are all steps towards even bigger wins. And keep the momentum going when you're on a roll – so if you're celebrating spending less money, don't do it by spending more money! And here's the best part: the more positive emotions you associate with money, the more likely you are to keep making good financial choices. Understanding these principles is the secret sauce to feeling confident and ready to tackle the juicier topics we'll cover later on, like borrowing and investing.

Why would I check my bank balance?
I don't need that kind of negativity
in my life.

Chapter 3
Facing your finances

Do you sometimes look at your bank balance and think, *where did all my money go?* Or panic in the checkout queue at the supermarket, hoping your card doesn't get declined? Is the end of the month always a struggle, no matter what? You're not the only one – 53% of people say they run out of money before payday, at least some of the time.[1] The good news? Monzo customers who look at their balance more than 10 times a month are 50% less likely to hit that empty-wallet moment.[2] Think 10 times sounds like a lot? The average person looks at their phone every 12 minutes.[3] If you can find the time to obsessively check the weather app, you can open your banking app a couple of times a week.

We're not saying you're a total ostrich when it comes to your money. Maybe this is basic stuff for you. But if this chapter just ends up being a well-deserved pat on the back, that's no bad thing!

Understanding your bank balance

Regularly checking your balance is like going to the gym. Once you get into a good routine, it makes you stronger. Eventually, you might even enjoy it! But starting is the hardest part. 'Money avoidance' is a real thing, and it works like this: you feel embarrassed and worried about the state of your finances, so you completely ignore them, and then continue spending (sometimes even more) to trick yourself into feeling good again. Like that exercise bike you bought but totally didn't need, it's a cycle.

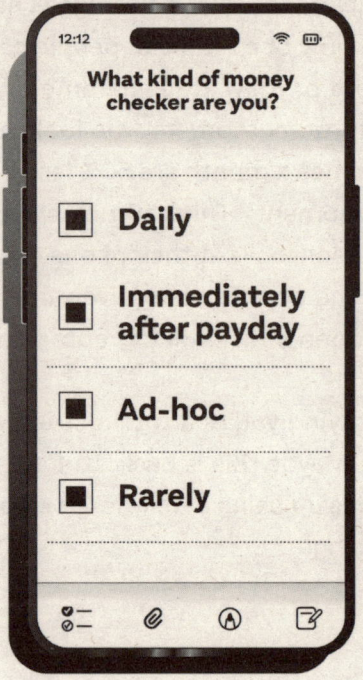

What type of money checker are you?

Daily: you like to stay on top of things. If you've got a lot of bills or run a household, small expenses can add up fast so keeping an eye on your bank balance helps you feel in control.

Immediately after payday: you start the month off right by saying a quick 'hello' to your hard-earned cash, and use this moment to top up your savings and budget for essentials before any spending sprees begin.

Ad hoc: you check in on an as-and-when basis, depending on what's going on in your life. Some of our customers say they often do this towards the end of the month if they're worried about going into their overdraft and want to avoid fees.

Rarely: you avoid looking at your balance because you're either confident about your spending, or anxious about what you'll see. Whether you're relaxed or worried, you'll always benefit from taking a peek more often.

If you're already a regular money-checker, a round of applause for you. Everyone else, it's time to start flexing those thumbs a bit more. Not only will regular check-ins help you get on top of your spending, they can also boost your savings, as you'll get better at spotting places you can cut back or put a little something extra aside. Set reminders, put it in your calendar, and add it to the 'life admin' list. And don't forget to reward yourself afterwards – a snack, a coffee, or an episode of your favourite show can turn this chore into something you actually look forward to.

Understanding your spending habits

Ever wondered exactly how much money you're spending on bills or bottles of olive oil? Grouping your spending into categories helps you spot patterns over time. Once you have a clear idea of where your money's actually going, you'll probably find there are things you can easily improve without much effort. And there are banking apps that'll do the categorising for you.

To start, try to track as close to 100% of your spending as possible. If you get paid weekly or fortnightly, adjust your tracking to match. As well as your current account, don't forget to include:

- Any other bank accounts
- Savings accounts or ISAs
- Credit cards
- Loans and finance repayment plans
- Any other overdrafts
- Money down the back of the sofa

Some banking apps let you add all your cards and accounts, even if they're with other banks. This is a great way to look at the big picture, and saves you from doing mental maths (or, worse still, creating a spreadsheet).

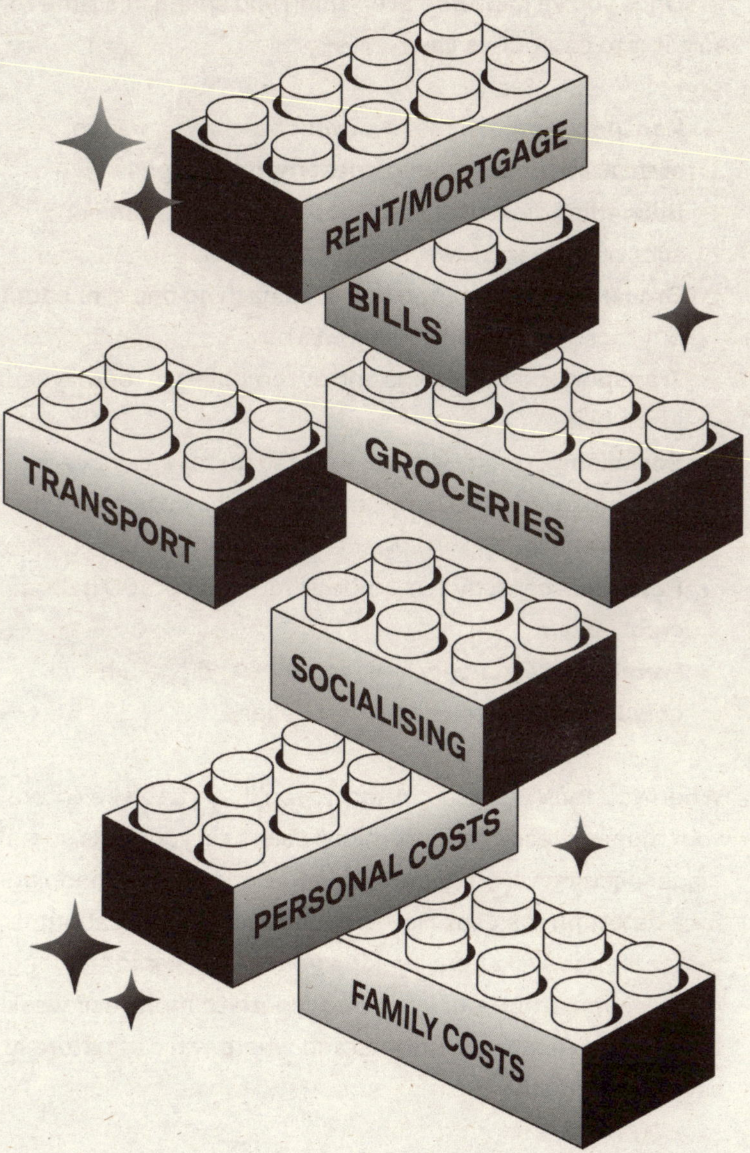

Once you've captured everything you spend, it's time to sort it into categories like:

- **Rent/mortgage:** a roof over your head and a wall to stare at? Probably your biggest monthly expense
- **Bills:** think electricity, internet and that random subscription you always forget to cancel
- **Groceries:** like that one bag of spinach no one ever eats, but for some reason you *have* to buy
- **Transport:** planes, trains and automobiles . . . or maybe just a bike
- **Socialising:** great, Jessica wants to go to Antarctica for her hen do (and the fluffy cowboy hat she expects you to wear is extra)
- **Personal costs:** gym membership, books or 100 balls of crochet yarn
- **Family costs:** nursery fees, zoo trips and enough colouring books to open an art gallery

When you look at each category, you'll start to see where your money's really going. It might even help you make some bigger decisions, like buying a train season ticket or shopping for a better phone deal. However you want to think about it, remember: it's all about making your life easier in the long run. By comparing your spending month to month, or week to week, you'll start to understand where you can naturally save or spend smarter.

Case study

'My impulse spending on little treats was getting out of control.'

Nadia, 34, is a project manager with a passion for cooking. Her job is pretty full on and she's always juggling multiple tasks and deadlines. On the days Nadia goes into the office, she treats herself to lunch from an Italian deli round the corner with some of her team. She also fuels up on their takeaway macchiatos before meetings and picks up ingredients to try out at home – think hand-rolled pasta, posh pesto, cheeses and artisanal chocolate.

Nadia's landlord recently put her rent up, and now her money just doesn't last as long. She's had several close calls at the checkout and has been running low on cash in the lead-up to payday. To get a handle on things, she knows she'll have to start keeping a closer eye on her outgoings. Crowdsourcing tips from friends and social media, she discovered a whole new way of managing her money.

Nadia's journey

1. **Checking daily:** Nadia started checking her account daily (usually with one eye closed). Seeing her bank balance at the start of each day reminded her exactly where she was at. No more burying her head in the sand!

2. **Using categories:** Nadia switched to a banking app that automatically sorted her spending into categories. After two months, she started to realise how much her deli trips were adding. She was spending up to £50 a week on treats!

3. **Setting boundaries:** once Nadia was clear on where her money was going, she set herself a limit of £30 a month on gourmet treats, and did the rest of her grocery shopping at a budget-friendly supermarket. She also set boundaries at work and only said yes to one team lunch a fortnight.

4. **Thinking twice:** the hardest step? Learning to pause before making a purchase. For every must-have ingredient, she started asking herself: '*Do I really need this?*', '*Will it improve my pasta sauce that much?*' She was surprised to find that more often than not the answer was no.

Nadia's now a self-proclaimed 'recovering impulse spender'. The bonus? She's now got space in her budget to put aside money for a foodie holiday to Italy. Bravissimo!

Keeping an eye on money coming into your account

If you have money that lands in your bank account regularly, it might come from a few different places. There are two things to keep in mind here: *when* it comes in, and *where* it comes

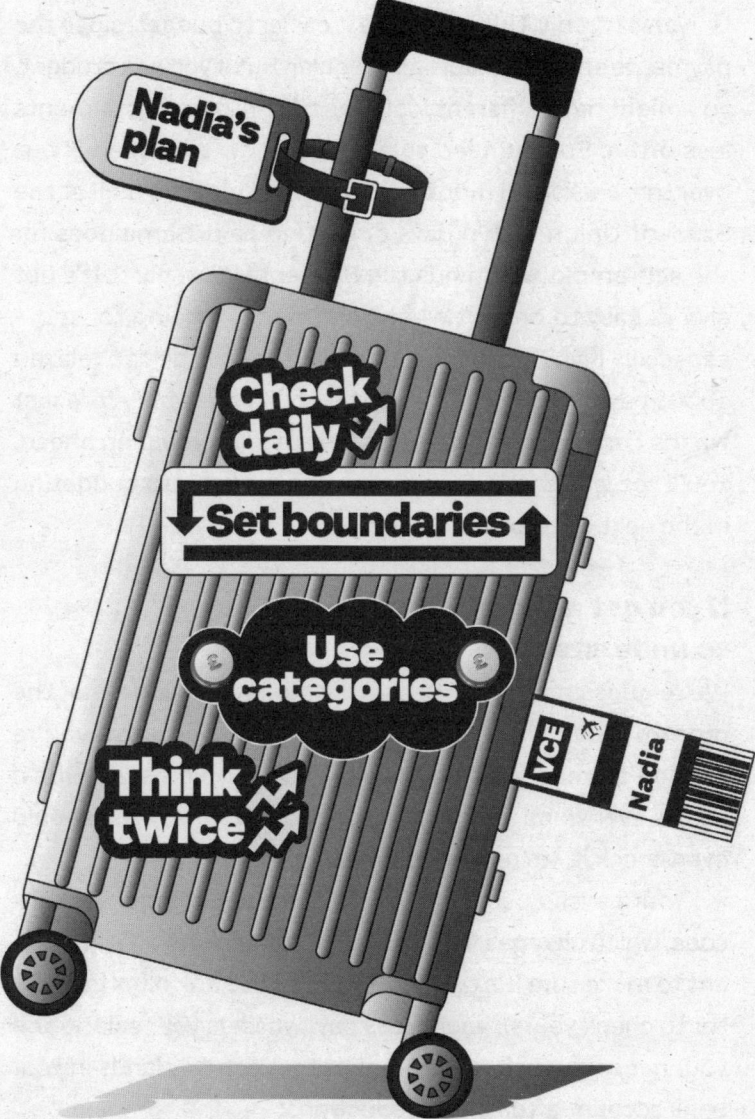

from. If you're paid through a monthly salary or benefits like Universal Credit, this can make it easier to budget, since the payments are predictable and regular. But if you're a student, you might have different loans landing in larger instalments less often. So you need to work out how to spread it out over the weeks and months, rather than blowing it all at the Student Union within days of getting paid. Same goes for the self-employed (minus the Student Union part). It's not always easy to predict when your money's going to land – especially if you work for clients who are a little too relaxed about paying you on time. But if you can roughly forecast what's coming in and when, it'll really help you plan ahead. You'll see why that's important when we get into budgeting in the next chapter.

If you get a payslip, it pays to understand it

We're guessing payday is one of your favourite days of the month. We're also guessing that it's not because you're excited to read your payslip in microscopic detail. But if you've ever wondered what it all means and why you should even check it, we're here to break it down.

Your payslip usually tells you three key things: your *tax code*, which changes with your circumstances (so it's important to make sure it's correct – you can use an online calculator to check yours); your *gross pay*, which is your salary; and your *net pay*, which is the amount that actually lands in your bank account after these deductions:

- **Income tax:** this may also appear as 'PAYE tax' on your payslip, meaning 'Pay As You Earn'. Income tax is calculated in bands, which are based on how much you earn. If you've not worked a full tax year – it runs from 6 April to 5 April – you might qualify for a lower band.

- **National Insurance contributions:** another kind of tax. You pay National Insurance to qualify for certain benefits and your state pension. Like income tax, the amount you pay depends on what you earn.

- **Pension contributions:** if you're eligible – aged between 22 and state pension age, and earning above £10,000 per year – you should be auto-enrolled into your workplace pension. In many cases, your employer will match some or all of your contributions. This can be a tax-efficient way of saving towards retirement. We'll cover this in detail in the 'Life after work' chapter.

- **Student loan payments:** if you're repaying a student loan, your employer might take the money directly out of your salary to give to the Student Loans Company. It all depends on what you earn (more on this in the 'Borrowing and debt' chapter).

- **Court orders and child maintenance:** your employer might have to take money directly from your pay for things like unpaid fines, debt repayments and child maintenance.

- **Workplace benefits:** some employers offer loans for things like rail season tickets. They'll usually take the repayments directly from your earnings.

- **Benefits in kind:** these are 'non-cash benefits'; perks like company cars, private healthcare and gym memberships. Your employer will pay for these benefits on your behalf, but they're taxable. For example, if you sign up to private health insurance provided by your company, your employer will pay the premiums but you'll pay the tax on it.

- **Salary sacrifice:** this is where you and your employer agree to give up part of your salary in exchange for non-cash benefits like pension contributions, cycle to work or technology schemes. Because salary sacrifice exchanges salary for a benefit, you might end up paying less tax and National Insurance.

- **Payroll giving:** this scheme lets you donate to charity directly from your pay.

You'll never be mystified by your payslip again!

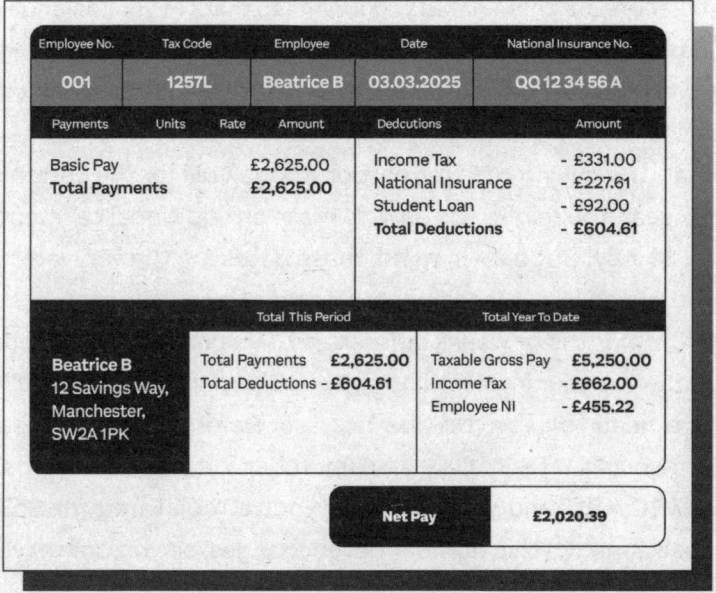

Employee No.	Tax Code	Employee	Date	National Insurance No.
001	1257L	Beatrice B	03.03.2025	QQ 12 34 56 A

Payments	Units	Rate	Amount	Dedcutions	Amount
Basic Pay			£2,625.00	Income Tax	- £331.00
Total Payments			£2,625.00	National Insurance	- £227.61
				Student Loan	- £92.00
				Total Deductions	- £604.61

	Total This Period		Total Year To Date	
Beatrice B 12 Savings Way, Manchester, SW2A 1PK	Total Payments £2,625.00 Total Deductions - £604.61		Taxable Gross Pay £5,250.00 Income Tax - £662.00 Employee NI - £455.22	

Net Pay	£2,020.39

A summary for the self-employed

If you've chosen to be your own boss that means you're in charge of your own lunch breaks. But it also means you're in charge of your own taxes. While your PAYE friends breeze through life without knowing when the tax year starts or ends, you spend January having vivid dreams about drowning in a pile of receipts. The basics are the same – you still owe the same taxes as PAYE employees – but *you're* the one responsible for putting aside the right amount. You can stay on track by replicating the PAYE system; putting the money in a separate pot as soon as you get paid, so you don't accidentally spend it. Some business bank accounts even do this for you!

There are three dates you'll want to mark in your calendar in bright red ink: **5 October,** which is the deadline for telling HMRC you need to complete a tax return. **31 January**, which is the deadline for paying any remaining tax for the last tax year, and paying the first part of your tax bill for the current tax year. You might also have to make an additional payment on **31 July**. But bear in mind, these dates are the very *latest* you can do all of these things. It's a good idea to do prep work a few months or weeks beforehand, like getting registered, gathering your invoices and calculating your expenses. You'll also need to get a 'Unique Taxpayer Reference', otherwise known as a UTR. It's like an ID number for your tax records. HMRC will send you one once you've registered for Self Assessment. (This number never changes, so you only have to do it once.)

If this all sounds like a lot, fear not! There's a group of people whose whole job it is to help you with this: accountants. They'll break down the steps you need to take and handle the maths. There's also information about how it all works on the Self Assessment section on the government website.[4]

Income protection

Income protection is a type of insurance policy that pays you a tax-free monthly income if you can't work for certain reasons, like illness or injury. While it won't necessarily match your entire monthly salary, it's designed to cover the essentials and help keep money worries at bay.

You can get this type of insurance whether you're salaried or self-employed. The amount you pay each month depends on your particular circumstances. Broadly speaking, the 'riskier' insurers see you as, the more expensive your policy is. So if you're a professional acrobat, you'll likely have to pay a higher premium than a writer who sits at a laptop all day. Other factors that'll impact the cost are things like your age, general health, any pre-existing conditions, and the length of your policy.

It's worth getting different quotes to see how your options compare, or speaking to a professional insurance broker.

Facing your Feed

130193 Treasury Terrace,
Goldenfields, GF9 2XP, United Kingdom

TAKEAWAYS

ITEM	QTY
Face your feed	1
Get to grips with your payslip	1
Create categories	1
TOTAL	**3**

HAVE A NICE DAY

TAKEAWAYS

Face your feed: the more you know, the more control you can have. Opening up your banking app daily will help you spot places where you could be spending less and saving more, as well as avoiding nasty surprises like overdraft fees.

Get to grips with your payslip: now you understand what everything means, check your payslip each month to make sure your tax code and deductions are correct. Or, if you're self-employed, stay on top of your invoices and make sure you're putting aside the right amount of tax each month.

Create categories: use an app to sort your spending into categories, so you can see exactly where your money goes. Setting up a system can make this simple to do, and the benefits can be huge. (We'll get into this again in the next chapter.)

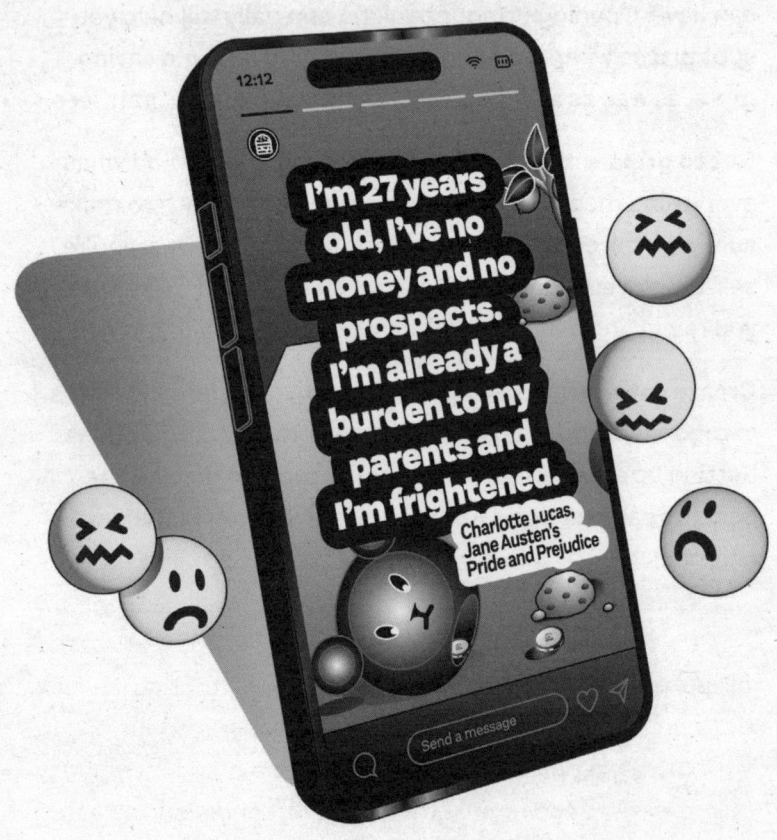

Chapter 4
Balancing your budget

Is there anything better than treating yourself to a payday spending spree? Or anything worse than passing up a night out in an attempt to be sensible? Budgeting can feel like an endless series of choices that mean you're either having fun and feeling guilty about it, or being frugal and ending up extremely bored. When we asked 2,000 of our customers what they needed help with, it was a landslide for: 'managing and organising the money that comes into my account' (a roundabout way of saying: budgeting).

The thought of taking a closer look at your spending habits, and possibly deciding they have to change, might be off-putting. But a good budget isn't about restricting yourself or saying goodbye to the things you love. It's about giving your money a purpose. It'll mean you can plan for everyday bills, expenses and regular treats without ending up stressed before payday. Once you're in control of the everyday stuff, you can start thinking about how to create more space in your budget for that other category we talked about in the 'Principles for your money' chapter: your savings and investments.

How you spend and budget is the foundation you can build your future fund on. So even though it might be a bit dull to look at your incomings and outgoings in microscopic detail, it really can make a world of difference down the line. Once you've cracked how to budget, you'll start feeling like the CEO of your own life. You might even have enough left over for a nifty little power suit.

Sort it out

We already talked about how to track and categorise your spending in the last chapter. When it comes to budgeting, that's the first step. Next, it's time to start thinking about the difference between your *needs* and *wants*. Some are obvious – rent, food and bills? Definitely *needs*. But the *wants*? That's where things get tricky. After all, who are we to tell you that a weekly boxing class or a blueberry brioche from your favourite bakery aren't some of life's essentials?

As a rule of thumb, a want is something you could technically live without. But don't panic – that doesn't mean you have to! A good budget should help you make room for the things you enjoy. After all, it's important to prioritise having fun in the *now* as well as planning for the future. Budgeting is all about finding balance and being intentional.

Once you've separated out your *needs* and *wants,* it's time to list your possible *surprises*. By their very nature these are hard to predict. But it's a fact of life that every so often you'll have to pay for something unplanned, like an emergency vet visit or a broken boiler. They might also be happy surprises – birthday presents and friends' weddings can fall into this category, too. You've probably heard the term 'safety net' before (a pot of money to help you deal with emergency costs), but we'd like to introduce you to the idea of a 'fun fund' as well – creating much-needed space for celebrating, gifting and other joyful things.

The 50–30–20 rule

Now that you've separated your *needs* and your *wants*, it's time to budget for them. You can do this however feels right to you, but if you're not sure where to start, or haven't had a chance to track your spending yet, one tried-and-tested method is the 50–30–20 rule.

- 50% of your income goes to needs – like mortgage or rent, bills and groceries.
- 30% is for wants – like eating out, clothes and holidays.
- 20% goes towards your savings (including your safety net), investments and debt repayments. Generally speaking, the idea here is to prioritise paying off your debt over saving and investing if you don't have space for both – more on that in a few chapters.

If you live in an expensive city like London, or look after kids or elderly parents, you might prefer the 75–15–10 rule: 75% for needs, 15% for wants and 10% for savings. But the percentages aren't a hard and fast rule, it's just about getting in the habit of separating your income.

Dividing up your money like this could work perfectly for you straight out of the box, but it's likely that it'll need a bit of finessing over time. That's why it's best to spend an hour or so on your budget after every payday to make sure that you're ready for the month ahead.

The envelope method

Once you've got your budget sorted, how do you keep your money separate? Back in the day, people would divide cash into physical envelopes. Now, most people prefer to do it digitally using a banking app. It goes like this: you set up a pot for each budget category and separate your money into them at the start of the month, then only spend what's in each one. A method loved by money-saving gurus everywhere, it's gained a cult-like following because it's simple and helps you see how much you've got left to spend on certain things.

Here's how you can make the most out of the envelope method:

- **Set personalised categories:** start by defining your budget categories. The more personal, the better! Think about everything in your life: rent, bills, home improvements, holidays, clothes for your kids, clothes for your dog, new Lego – break it down as much as you like.

- **Allocate realistic amounts:** use the 50–30–20 rule as a guideline, or start with your 'savings' and 'needs' and see what's left over for 'wants'. Remember to be realistic. It's worth slightly overestimating for things like bills and groceries, and planning for annual costs like your car MOT. You might find it helpful to keep these annual expenses in separate pots, too.

- **Don't let big occasions catch you out:** we tend to budget on a monthly basis, but you'll likely have recurring costs that fall into the 'every now and again' bucket, like weddings and seasonal wardrobe upgrades. Have a think about what those are, and how much they (roughly) add up to, then give them a separate envelope you contribute to regularly.

- **Don't forget your insurance policies:** for some stuff, insurance is legally required, like insurance for your car. But for other wants and needs, you'll have the option of whether or not you want to add insurance on. Think holidays, phones, and phones you lose on holiday. Plus insurance for your four-legged friends. Don't forget to make an envelope for these things too.

- **Think long term:** you might have some specific longer term financial goals that fall either into the needs or wants categories. Give them their own envelopes and contribute to them every month, even if you're not spending yet.

- **Use digital envelopes:** while physical envelopes work, there are plenty of apps that will let you set up digital pots or folders. You can sometimes even automate the process by assigning direct debits to specific pots.

Remember, no matter how well you plan, life changes so your budget should too. Check your categories regularly and update them as often as you need.

Case study

'I have a good job and a steady income. Why do I end up in my overdraft each month?'

Tomasz, 30, is a history teacher who loves music festivals and nights out (and a cheeky kebab afterwards). He's always up for a good time, but his wallet? Not so much. He feels overwhelmed by his finances, unsure about how much he should be saving and often dipping into his overdraft towards the end of the month.

One day, while secretly scrolling under his desk during a class test, Tomasz read about the 50–30–20 rule. Could this be the answer to enjoying his weekends without the spending shame spiral? He decided it was worth a shot.

After doing some maths, Tomasz found the 50–30–20 split too restrictive because of his high rent. So he tried the 75–15–10 split instead.

With a monthly net income of £1,900, he divided up his budget like this:

1. Needs (75%) £1,425: rent, bills, groceries and transport

2. Wants (15%) £285: festivals, seeing friends, eating out

3. Savings and debt repayment (10%) £190: creating a safety net and paying off his overdraft

Tomasz's map
THE 75–15–10 SPLIT

CASE STUDY: LESSONS IN BUDGETING

📍 **MONTHLY INCOME**   £1,900

75% **NEEDS:**
Rent, bills, groceries and transport   £1,425

15% **WANTS:**
Festivals, seeing friends and eating out   £285

10% **SAVINGS & DEBT REPAYMENT:**
Creating a safety net
and paying off his overdraft   £190

Tomasz checked in on his budget every payday, immediately separating his needs, wants, debt repayments and savings into different pots, so his money wouldn't get mixed up. He also set up direct debits for his bills so there was one less thing to think about.

Once Tomasz knew he had £285 a month to spend on whatever he liked, he felt more relaxed. One month he spent £50 on gig tickets and put the rest towards nights out with friends. Another month, he used all of it for a weekend away to Barcelona. Having a limit stopped Tomasz unknowingly overspending on wants before he'd covered all his needs – and meant he could actually enjoy himself guilt-free.

Spending less

Laying your spending out might have you saying *'wait, how on earth am I paying £400 a year for my phone bill?!'* With a little research and planning, you might be able to trim these kinds of costs without too much effort.

- **Price comparison sites are your new best friend:** who needs 500GB of data every month? Unless you're running a YouTube channel from a remote island, probably not you. Check out comparison sites to find a plan you'll actually use.

- **Beware of hidden fees:** roaming fees and out-of-contract charges are examples of ninja expenses – silently chopping away at your budget. Always read your contract to find out how the costs break down.

- **Master the art of the swap:** if you can travel off-peak, would it save you money on train tickets? Can you *really* tell the difference between hand-churned yoghurt and the regular stuff? Probably not, but your bank account can. Little swaps like these can add up fast.

- **No-spend days to the rescue:** pick a few days each month when you vow not to spend a penny. It's like giving your wallet a spa day. Not only will it help to balance out those days when you seem to spend £30 just by leaving your house, but it'll also make you feel really smug.

- **Review your subscriptions:** it's easy to lose track of how many services you're paying for – Sky, Netflix, Spotify Premium, Prime and who knows what else. Take a good look at what you actually use and consider downgrading or cutting back. Sometimes when you try to cancel, they'll immediately offer you a better deal. You might decide it now fits in your budget, or that you don't really need it at all.

Fight the impulse

So you've done the hard work. Your spending is tracked, your budget is balanced and your savings look healthy. And then, disaster strikes. You're walking down the high street when suddenly, there it is, begging you to buy it: a brand new gold chrome XL air fryer. The ultimate upgrade. You didn't plan to buy it, but you really, really want to.

Here's how to keep those impulse buys in check:

- **Delay the decision:** many retailers want you to believe that if you don't buy *right now*, you'll miss out on the deal of a lifetime. It's not true – sales are always happening. So try to walk away. You might find that the impulse cools off, but if not, that air fryer (or whatever shiny new thing you *have* to have) will most likely still be there when you come back.

- **Think about bigger savings:** remember, if you don't buy it, you save 100% of the cost. That's just maths. If you're not buying the latest gadget, you're keeping that cash in your pocket for something you'll enjoy more down the line, like a holiday, a boosted savings balance, or just making the run-up to payday feel smoother.

- **Remember your long-term goals:** your monthly income isn't infinite (unless you've won the lottery or your side hustle is suddenly booming). So if you buy the new air fryer, you'll probably have to sacrifice something else. Is it really worth it? Or will that dopamine hit wear off after 15 minutes when you realise it's basically exactly the same as the one you already have?

Staying motivated

The trick to sticking to a budget is to keep things rewarding and full of little wins along the way. Here are some ideas for turning budgeting into something you'll enjoy:

- **Gamify your goals:** turn your finances into fun by setting mini challenges for yourself. For example, see if you can go a month without getting a takeaway (while treating yourself to some new ingredients to try at home). If you've got a particular long-term goal in mind, you could use those primary school art skills and make a chart to track how close you are to smashing your target. Even if it's silly, if it makes you feel good, it's worth it.

- **Start a friendly competition:** saving can feel more like a sport when you turn it into a competitive game with a friend, partner or family member. Set a group challenge to see who can save the most by the end of the month (we've got some fun examples in the 'Strategies for saving' chapter). A little rivalry might be exactly the push you need to hit your goals.

- **Treat yourself:** budgeting doesn't mean you have to live like a monk. Give yourself a treat when you hit a milestone. The secret is to plan this into your budget, so you can indulge guilt-free.

Budgeting

030384 Treasury Terrace,
Goldenfields, GF9 2XP, United Kingdom

TAKEAWAYS

ITEM	QTY
Give your money a purpose	1
Keep your budget true to life	1
Expect the unexpected	1
TOTAL	**3**

TAKEAWAYS

Give your money a purpose: a budget helps you be intentional about how you use your money – so create a plan that accounts for your hobbies, treats and things you enjoy, as well as future planning and everyday essentials.

Keep your budget true to life: be as specific and personal as possible. If your circumstances change, your budget should too.

Expect the unexpected: whether it's a spontaneous camping trip or a visit to the dentist, try to create a budget that leaves room for unplanned situations – the good and the bad.

Chapter 5
Doing money together

Money is something we share, but that doesn't mean everyone feels the same way about it. Throughout your life, you become connected to more and more people. You'll be financially responsible for some of them, and others you'll have to share money with. From friends and flatmates to partners and children, you'll have to work out how to 'do money' with lots of different people – so it's worth figuring out how to do it well.

Money and friends

You're at a restaurant with a friend when the bill arrives. You assumed you were splitting everything equally, but your friend starts combing through it, item by item. You learn that you had two more drinks than they did. They didn't have any sides. And they don't believe in tipping. Suddenly, it's like you don't know them at all. Or maybe you're sitting at home on a Saturday night, curry on the way, ready to binge-watch a new dating show where 12 hot singles are stranded in a shark-infested ocean until they find true love . . . when the loading wheel of death kicks in. Uh-oh, the broadband has been cut off. Your flatmate had assumed *you* were paying for it, because they cover Netflix, but you thought *they* were paying for it because you buy all the milk. And they drink so much milk. 'How much milk can a person digest?' you wonder. You try to google it but you can't, because there's no Wi-Fi.

Friends and money can be a weird combination. Everyone has different attitudes and budgets, and you can't always predict how things will go. It gets even more complex as you get older and lives go in different directions – some friends will be taking a pay cut for a career change, others will be saving for a wedding, and some might be starting a family or taking on financial responsibility for elderly parents. The way to make friends and money feel easier – at any life stage – is by being upfront. Too often, we dance around the topic of money so delicately that even knowing what someone is asking for can be a challenge. It's all 'no worries if not' and 'at your earliest convenience'. You'd need to be a mind reader to understand that Greg wants his fiver back RIGHT NOW, even though he told you 'it wasn't urgent' an hour ago. Luckily, a quick 'shall we split this down the middle?' or 'this is on me, you get the next one' can save you a lifetime of awkwardness.

The potential for drama multiplies when you go on holiday with friends, because you're doing *all* the things at once: sharing meals, drinks, taxis and grocery shops. It's easy to start stressing out, especially if your friends earn more money than you, or if they're a bit too enthusiastic about how many tapas they're ordering. Skip the tension entirely by deciding before the trip how you plan to manage your shared expenses and how much you each want to spend. And don't do this in the departure lounge – set time aside to have this chat before you even book your flights. There are lots of practical ways to

share travel costs, like each putting physical currency in a group wallet (otherwise known as a 'kitty'). This technique is an oldie but a goodie. Or, if you're worried about carrying cash around, there are apps that do a similar thing. You can add expenses, track what you've each spent, and keep an eye on the running total. And most will do the maths for you when you're ready to settle up. Now *that's* a holiday.

Being upfront about shared expenses is one thing, but getting people to actually pay you back is another. Sharing account details and setting up a new payee is a faff, while chasing friends for money undoes all the relaxing you did while drifting around on a lilo. Tech can help here, too, as many banking apps let you create handy payment links and even send reminders to friends for you. But no matter how organised you are, there's always that one person who wants to keep the holiday spirit going by never settling up. Before you turn into a full-time debt collector, here are a couple of things you could try:

- **Agree on a deadline:** give everyone a specific date to work towards.
- **Say thanks:** thank people for paying you back in the group chat. It's a gentle reminder to anyone who hasn't paid yet that doesn't require any nagging.
- **Break it up:** if you feel like a friend's dragging their heels because they don't have the cash, you could check if

they're OK and come to an agreement, like paying half now and half later (if you can afford it).

- **Set an example:** remember, respect goes both ways. Make sure you're paying your friends back on time, too.

As long as everyone's happy with how you've agreed to do things, money shouldn't be a barrier to friendship.

Case study

'Love living with mates. Hate doing household admin.'

Meet Adé. He's 24, a graphic designer and, if we're honest, a bit disorganised.

Living with two equally chaotic friends in a flat in Edinburgh seemed like a dream, until Adé became the 'unofficial treasurer'. You know, when you pay for everything upfront, and hope your friends will pay you back? Well, that didn't happen. From splitting the electricity bill, to chipping in for pizza, or covering the Apple TV subscription, somehow Adé always ended up out of pocket, sending panicky 3am texts after realising his bank account was empty again. He needed to figure out how to ask his friends to pay him back on time without constantly nagging them.

Here's what he did:

- **The one app rule:** sick of sending last-minute 'can you pay me back?' texts whenever he randomly remembered, Adé and his flatmates agreed to stick to one banking app for all their expenses. For day-to-day spending, they used a bill-splitting feature to track their spending and pay each other back. And for bigger things like household bills, they finally got around to setting up direct debits.
- **Fridge whiteboard:** no more shoving unopened post in a drawer. It was time to put all the regular bills where everyone could see them, each time they reached for the orange juice.
- **Settle-up Sunday:** Adé and his flatmates agreed to hang out and have dinner together on the last Sunday of every month. They used the time to settle any outstanding bills, check all their house admin was up to date, and hash out any burning grievances over a pizza.

Adé soon found his bank account was looking healthier, and there was no more awkward tension in the flat.

01
THE ONE APP RULE

02
FRIDGE WHITEBOARD

✳ Adé's
**bill
break
down**

03
SETTLE-UP SUNDAY

££
HAVE FUN

Money and romance

Talking about money with a new flame sits somewhere between 'putting your cold feet on your partner in bed' and 'forcing them to spend Christmas with your annoying cousin' on a list of the biggest romantic buzzkills. That's one reason why the honeymoon period feels so sweet – when you first start dating someone, your money is totally separate from theirs. You don't know how much they earn. You don't know how much they have in savings. And unless you're doing some deep-state-level stalking, you definitely don't know their credit score. Honestly, you might not even know their full name. And that's your business. Who are we to judge?

Dating is expensive and working out who pays for what on a first date can feel awkward. But if things go well and your star signs align, you'll enter the wild, heady heyday of sharing, gifting and treating one another. Yes, Leo and Aries are a perfect match, and he makes a mean spaghetti bolognese, but for love to truly last, you've got to be on the same page about money. So when is the right time to start talking about your finances? Somewhere between the third date and moving in together is perfect. Seriously, do it then, while you still find each other irresistibly charming for absolutely no reason. Don't wait until you're paying for things like rent, cars, kids and pets.

It's less about knowing the exact numbers right away and more about understanding each other's values and life goals. In a new relationship, start small, perhaps with a light question like *'do you buy a coffee every day?'*, which can open up a conversation about daily spending without any pressure. As you get more comfortable, you can move on to slightly deeper questions like *'how many credit cards do you have?'*, which can tell you about their approach to debt and money management. Finally, when you're building a life together, you can unlock more serious conversations, like *'are you planning on buying a house, and is that something you'd want to do together?'* At this point, it's about making sure you're ready to tackle the future as a team.

During these conversations, you might find that you have different attitudes and goals. According to our research,

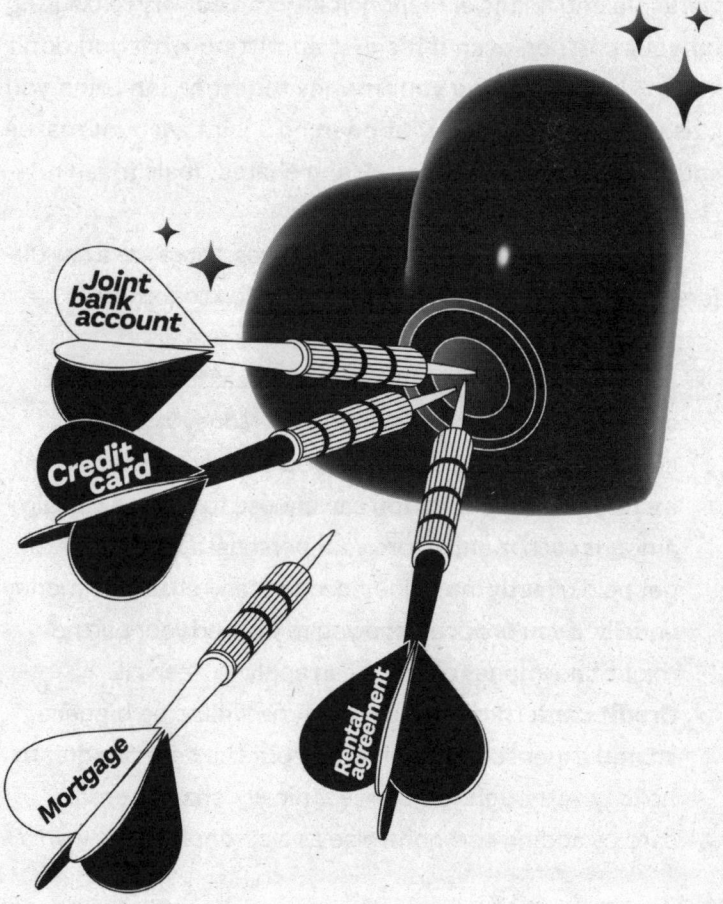

many couples in the UK feel this way – 3.4 million said they didn't think they were financially compatible with their partner.[1] It's not the end of the world, but it can create tension down the line if you don't keep an eye on it. As tough as these conversations can be, if you go in with an open mind, you'll probably feel much lighter and happier afterwards. Taking financial responsibility can be very reassuring for your partner, even if it's just admitting what you don't know. Plus, managing your money together can bring you closer. Research shows that opening a joint account makes couples feel more connected, and shared goals mean relationships last longer.[2]

If you do decide to share your finances, there are a few different ways your money might end up tied together:

- **Joint bank account:** these can be great for things like shared savings and household bills. Money in a joint account will belong to both of you equally, no matter how much you each put in. You can choose to pay in a certain amount each month from your personal accounts, or to get paid directly into a joint account and share the money equally. If you break up and you're worried your partner might take money out, you can apply to freeze it.
- **Credit card:** these can be handy for financing bigger shared expenses, like spreading out the cost of a dream holiday. Although you can technically 'share' a credit card by adding someone else as a cardholder, it's worth

remembering that the account holder is the person who has control. They can take the cardholder off and close the account.

- **Mortgage:** many couples have a joint mortgage, which means both people are responsible for it. You should let your lender know if there are any changes to your circumstances.
- **Rental agreement:** these are like mortgages; if you're both named on the agreement, you're both responsible for it.

Just remember, while there are emotional and practical advantages to tying your money together, there are possible risks, too. For example, your partner's credit score will become linked to yours as soon as you open a bank account together. Not sure why that matters? Check out the 'Borrowing and debt' chapter! Moving in with someone can also affect some of the benefits you're entitled to. This is because you have to claim all *income-based* benefits as a couple. So, say for example you claimed Universal Credit as a single person, if you moved in with your partner and earned too much combined, you wouldn't qualify any more. If you claim benefits, you should check the government website to see how these kinds of lifestyle changes could impact you. Ultimately, when it comes to the matter of sharing money, the key is to do your homework, and make sure you really trust the person you're sharing with.

Life insurance

Life insurance can pay out a lump sum to whoever you choose (also known as a 'beneficiary') if you pass away. It's not a nice thing to think about, but it can give you comfort and peace of mind to know your loved ones won't be left without any support if something happens. This is even more important to consider if you have kids. Just remember to check whether your workplace offers this as a benefit before you pay out for a private policy.

Money and marriage

Marriage isn't on the cards for everyone, particularly if you hate planning parties, wearing white or watching your uncle dance to 'Mr Brightside' with a tie on his head. But if you do decide to get married, it's important to know how it'll impact your finances.

Chances are, if you've been with your partner a long time, you already live together, share a credit card, or have a joint bank account. So you might find that getting married doesn't change a whole lot when it comes to your money, but there are a few things you should look into. First up, you might become entitled to certain tax benefits. Some married couples and civil partners qualify for something called a Marriage Allowance. This is a government scheme that lets a lower-earning spouse transfer up to 10% of their unused personal allowance to their partner, which can reduce the higher earning spouse's tax, and therefore your overall bills. Always get advice from an accountant for the latest, as rules change. You may also be able to get more out of your workplace benefits once you get married. For example, some employers will let you add your spouse to your private healthcare plan. Speak to your HR department to find out if this is something they offer.

A lot of the other big changes are related to things that'll most likely impact you in older age, like your pension and will. If you live in England or Wales and had a will from before you got married, it becomes void once you say *I do*, so you might want to think about making a new one, otherwise your belongings will be shared out according to 'the rules of intestacy'. This is a law that determines who gets what when you die, which might not follow your wishes. In terms of your pension, you could be entitled to your partner's pension when they pass away, but it depends on the type of pension and the specific scheme. Check out the government website for the latest rules on this or speak to your provider.

Even though divorce rates are dropping, break-ups still happen, so it's a good idea to be prepared; if only because the more deeply your money is connected, the more admin you'll have to do if you separate. Money might be the last thing on your mind during a stressful time like this, but it's important to make sure that your joint assets and liabilities are handled the right way.

Ultimately, money is an inevitable part of all relationships, whether you're dating, cohabiting, married or divorced. In any case, it's good to get ahead of the conversation. It can even be a litmus test for the strength of your communication. If you're already working on managing your money together, you should be proud!

Case study

'We don't split the rent equally, but in our case that's only fair.'

Meet Bea, a 52-year-old editor who's just moved in with her partner Lizze, 54, who earns about £19,000 a year more than she does.

If they split their rent 50/50, it'll mean Bea has a lot less disposable income than Lizze to spend on the things she wants. So to keep things fair and balanced, they've decided to split their monthly rent based on their earnings. That way, they'll both have the same proportion of money left over at the end of each month to spend on their own hobbies: Bea likes high-intensity spin classes, while Lizze prefers to lounge in a sauna. Look, it works for them.

Here's the sum they used:

1. They added up the total of both of their monthly incomes after deductions (their 'take home' pay).

2. They calculated their shares of the rent by dividing their individual incomes by the total household income.

Here's how it worked in practice:
- Bea earns £2,000 per month

- Lizze earns £3,000 per month
- Their total combined income is £5,000 per month
- Bea's share is 2000 ÷ by 5,000 = 0.4, or 40% of the rent
- Lizze's share is 3000 ÷ by 5,000 = 0.6, or 60% of the rent

The couple didn't want their salary difference to get in the way of moving in together. By splitting their rent this way, they both felt comfortable with what they were spending. And for Bea especially, it was a big weight off her shoulders.

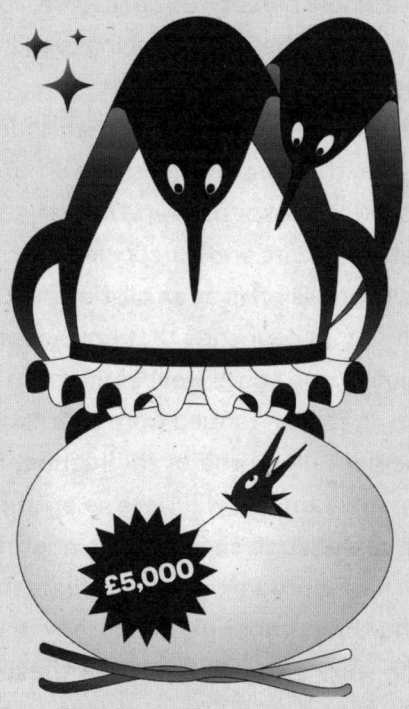

Money and kids

Kids are probably the biggest emotional and financial investment you'll ever make. And like any great investment, there's plenty to look forward to – first words, adorably sticky fingers, graduations, tantrums. And while it's common knowledge your finances change hugely when you have kids, not knowing what those costs add up to is a source of anxiety for lots of people. The average cost of raising a child to the age of 18 in the UK is estimated at around £260,000 for a couple, and £290,000 for a single parent.[3] But of course, you don't need that money upfront – these will be things you'll pay for gradually over time.

You might think teens are pricier than toddlers if you're a first-timer, but the cost of the latest iPhone is actually dwarfed by childcare expenses in the early years. That's because private childcare and nursery fees are at an all-time high, and public provision is at an all-time low. In 2022, the OECD (a forum of 38 countries that promotes practices to improve economic and social wellbeing) estimated that net childcare costs in the UK ranged from 5–25% of the average income[4] – incidentally, some of the highest in the world! That means many families will have to stump up cash for childcare, or make a tough choice about whether one parent stays home. This disproportionately affects mothers, with many reducing the number of hours[5] they're working, and 1 in 10 leaving work altogether.[6] While these are societal issues you can't control, no matter how frustrating they are, there are things you can do to help keep costs down. First, visit the government website to see if you're entitled to any benefits. If your child's between three and four, you could be entitled to 30 hours of free childcare a week. And because grandparents are increasingly involved in childcare, they might be entitled to some tax breaks too. There's also the 'Tax-Free Childcare' scheme, where you can get up to £2,000 a year per child to put towards costs. It's really worth checking to see what you can claim; although 1.3 million families are eligible for help, around 800,000 aren't claiming, most likely because they don't realise they qualify.[7] You can also save a lot on clothes and toys by leaning on hand-me-downs from friends, or scoring deals on second-hand sites like Vinted.

Once kids hit school age, expenses shift. Sure, there are school uniforms, new shoes and endless birthday parties, but there's also the advantage of school replacing the bulk of your childcare, hopefully freeing up a bit more of your time in the process. The teen years are where kids might start requesting pricier stuff, like laptops, smartphones and branded clothes. This is also when you can start teaching them about managing their own money, as they become more independent.

Take it one stage at a time, get help where you can, and know that not everything needs to be the most expensive version available. Parenting on a budget is possible, and plenty of families thrive with careful planning, a little creativity, and a realistic approach to what's really essential.

Teaching kids about money

It seems odd that we don't really learn about money at school when it's such a huge part of our adult lives. Then, when we become adults, we're surprised when we don't automatically know anything about interest rates or investments, like they're things we should have absorbed by osmosis. If you're a parent, you have a huge amount of influence over your kids' attitudes and values towards money. So much so that 88% of children say they would go to their parents or carers for advice about it![8] That means it's worth thinking about what habits you want them to learn – and which you don't. You'll probably find that kids are naturally curious about money, and willing to learn. After all, it's the gateway to sweets, small plastic toys and add-on packs for phone games called things like 'BRIDGESMASHER' or 'BIRDSLAM' that you'll never be able to understand.

The most practical way to begin this conversation is with pocket money, if that's something you want and are able to do. Not everyone gives their kids an allowance – only about 30% of UK parents do – but it's a great way to get them used to the idea of financial responsibility and the fact we often have to choose between multiple things we want. The average amount of pocket money for kids aged 8–16 is around £9 a week. Some parents pay this for doing chores, like washing the car, walking the dog or babysitting younger siblings, which is actually a really useful learning opportunity.

To help your kids understand the value of money, you could try equating each task with a set amount. That way they can see clearly how many chores they'll have to complete to afford those Roblox tokens they so desperately need. Of course, pocket money isn't a perfect analogy for adult life. After all, when else will you earn money for things – like making your bed or doing the dishes – that everyone else has to do for free? But expanding out their chores like this can hint at the reality of what working life might be like, and help them understand that they'll need to work for some of the things they want.

Junior bank accounts can help kids learn and budget, too. Most of them allow you to create saving goals, keep a close eye on their outgoings, and set spending limits. Some come with a debit card that teens can use themselves, which notifies you each time they spend. This can also be a handy way to check in on them while they're out and about. How many bubble teas can one 12-year-old drink? You're about to find out! Generally, these accounts are designed to grow with kids, so you can increase their financial independence as they get older.

Along with setting up a junior bank account they can use themselves, there are other types of account you can contribute to on your kids' behalf, to set money aside for the future. One is called a Junior Individual Savings Account (JISA), which is tax-free. They generally work in the same way as an ISA (which we cover in the 'Strategies for saving' chapter), but the allowance is smaller, at £9,000 per year for the 2024/2025 tax year. This can give you peace of mind that you're creating a cushion for your kids that'll support them as they venture into adulthood. There are also Junior SIPPs – pensions you can set up for your children, which they can't access until they retire. We'll cover this in detail in the 'Life after work' chapter.

Just remember that, with JISAs and most children's bank accounts, your kids will get full access to their money when they turn 18. So if they spend it all on a birthday trip to Ibiza, there's technically nothing you can do about it (except for letting out an exasperated sigh). All the more reason to talk about money with your kids, and consider giving them a taste of financial responsibility when they're younger.

Case study

'I came up with a plan to turn £80 a month into over £14,000 for my daughter.'

Meet Manpreet, a single parent to a dinosaur-obsessed seven-year-old named Jade.

Manpreet wants to be proactive and set aside money for Jade for when she turns 18 to use for university, a first car, or just to get her savings started. She's worked out that she can afford to put aside £80 a month, and wants to make sure she's getting the most from her money over a long-term period.

After doing some research, Manpreet learned that Jade's money could grow more if she invested it, but there was risk attached – a chance she could get back less than she put in (we'll cover this in detail in the 'Becoming an investor' chapter). She wanted to make the most of the returns investing could give her, but didn't want to risk *all* her money, so she decided to spread it between two different types of account: a savings account and a Junior Individual Savings Account (JISA), which was invested in stocks and shares.

Here's how she split her contributions, and the totals she ended up with:

Savings account

- Manpreet's monthly contribution: £30
- Interest rate: 2%
- Over 11 years, her contributions will total £3,960
- With the 2% interest *and* compound interest, this could grow to about £4,800 by the time Jade turns 18

JISA

- Manpreet's monthly contribution: £50

- Estimated annual return: 4%
- Over 11 years, her contributions will total £6,600
- With compound returns, this could grow to about £9,800 by the time Jade turns 18. But Manpreet kept in mind that her returns *could* be less than this because of the risks involved with investing money

Combined, these savings could give Jade around £14,600 – not a bad 18th birthday present!

When it comes to saving for children, the earlier you start, the better. And by contributing a little whenever you can, you'll be surprised how much it'll add up.

THE TOOTH FAIRY FUND

To Jade:

Happy 18th birthday!

£14,600.00

Tooth Fairy

MONEY TOGETHER

2805 Lovers' Lane,
Goldenfields, GF9 2XP, United Kingdom

TAKEAWAYS

ITEM	QTY
Talk about it!	1
Plan, plan, plan	1
Set an example	1
Get ahead of big changes	1
TOTAL	4

HAVE A NICE DAY

TAKEAWAYS

Talk about it!: we don't talk about money enough. Whether it's with your partner, friends or kids, communication is everything. Being honest about your feelings can prevent misunderstandings down the line. And that goes both ways – listen to what others have to say about money, too.

Plan, plan, plan: when you're sharing money – for household bills, a holiday or even just splitting dinner – think ahead about how you want it to work. Agreeing upfront how you'll track and split costs can save you from stress later on.

Set an example: think about how you like to be treated when money's on the table, and do the same for your friends. Be considerate of their situation, respect their suggestions and pay them back on time.

Get ahead of big changes: moving in together, getting married or having children can have a big impact on your finances. Do some research or speak to a financial adviser so you know how these milestones will affect your money. Future you will thank you for being prepared.

Part 2

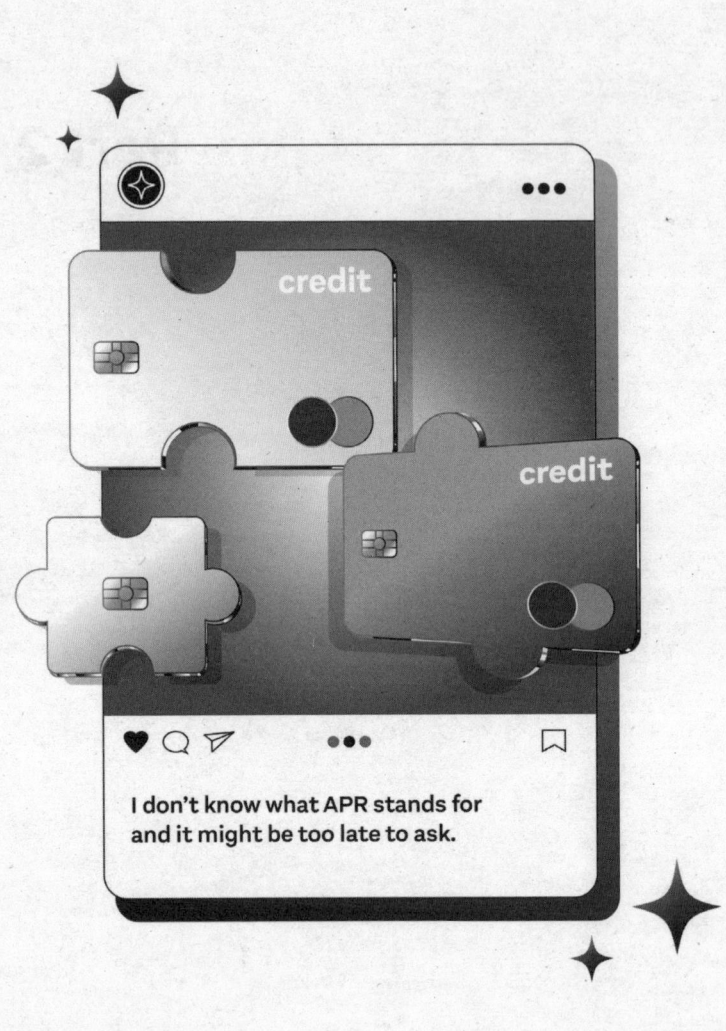

I don't know what APR stands for and it might be too late to ask.

Chapter 6
Borrowing and debt

Houses. Holidays. Cars. IOUs you scrawled on a sticky note when you broke into your older sibling's sweet stash. Without borrowing, many of life's big-ticket items would be stuck on the 'maybe one day' list. Debt might sound like a scary word, but it's the mortgage that helps someone buy their first home, the funding that turns a side hustle into an empire, and the student loan that helps start a career (or, at the very least, gives you a fancy degree worth framing).

At its best, debt is like a time machine that sends you money from the future to help you do something now. At its worst, it's a small win today that creates a huge problem tomorrow. Some of our customers say even the *thought* of debt makes them uncomfortable, because no matter how it's dressed up, it means you owe someone money. On top of that, you can buy pretty much anything on credit these days. It can be really hard to resist buying things you can't afford when you see beautiful, shiny people on social media living perfectly curated lives. The key thing is to borrow *intentionally*, because debt doesn't have to be the villain of your financial story. It can be your supportive, useful sidekick – the Robin to your Batman – if you use it right.

So before we get into how you can be more intentional about how you borrow, let's look at where you are now. Everyone has a different comfort zone when it comes to borrowing money, and taking a closer look at yours is a great place to start.

The comfort zone scale

Borrowing money responsibly can bring big life goals closer, so working out how you feel about being in debt is essential.

Low: this is you if . . .

- you've never borrowed before, so you're either curious about how debt could help you, or cautious about taking it on.
- you've struggled to pay off debt in the past – maybe you'll relate to the borrowing red flags we talk about later in this chapter.
- debt makes you nervous because it was a worry in your home growing up.

Medium: this is you if . . .

- you want to improve or maintain your credit score, so you've used debt for smaller things and were responsible about paying it off.
- you use your carefully collected credit card reward points to jet around the world, then not-so-humbly brag about it to friends and family.
- you've considered taking on bigger debt for longer-term commitments, but the thought of it might make you nervous. And you'd have to adjust your budget to make space for the repayments.

High: this is you if . . .

- you're the one in the friendship group people come to for advice on credit cards, interest rates and the small print on a loan.
- you know your stuff and love nothing more than shopping around for the best deal out there.
- you use debt to fund changes that match up to bigger life goals and priorities, like buying a home or car.
- you're top of the class when it comes to borrowing well, paying off your credit card on time, every time. You're confident you have the long-term stability to pay back what you've borrowed.

Eligibility and affordability

Before we dive into the details, let's start right at the very beginning. How do you even qualify for things like loans, credit cards and mobile phone contracts? How do lenders know you're trustworthy? How much interest do you owe your sibling for that bag of sweets you 'borrowed' 20 years ago?

There are two main things that lenders will consider before they approve you: eligibility and affordability.

Your *eligibility* depends on your age, your credit score (more on that in just a second), your income and financial history. Lenders use these to gauge whether you can pay them back.

Your *affordability* is based on whether you can repay the

money you borrow without struggling to cover your usual expenses, like rent, bills and food.

Lenders will always look at both, and you should too!

Everything you need to know about credit reports and scores

When you left school, you probably thought you'd left reports behind for ever. While your credit report won't tell your parents how bad you are at netball, it *will* give lenders a sense of how good you are at repaying what you've borrowed.

Your credit report tells them whether you've repaid loans on time, how much of your available credit you use, how long you've been using credit, the different types of credit you've managed, and how often you've applied to borrow money. All this data creates something that's kind of like a borrowing school report, with your grade being your *credit score*. The companies that collect and store this information are called credit bureaus. The major ones are Experian, Equifax and TransUnion, and some might charge for a more detailed view of your score. Each bureau might hold a different score for you, since they all get their data from different sources and carry out checks at different times. So to get the broadest idea of your credit health, it's a good idea to check all three.

Credit scores are one of those things that some people obsess over, some people fear, and others completely ignore. But what power does it really have? Basically, the better your credit score, the more options you have when trying to get credit or a loan. And if your credit score is low, you

The Lending Gazette

Dearest gentle borrowers,

Did you know that Experian started out as 'The Society of Guardians for the Protection of Tradesmen against Swindlers, Sharpers and other Fraudulent Persons'? It was founded all the way back in 1826 in Manchester.

Its members – mostly business owners and shopkeepers – received a monthly leaflet with information on people who'd failed to pay their debts. The scandal!

They collected the information from people who lived in the city, and so it was prone to hearsay and gossip – people's creditworthiness was basically reliant on their reputation. Unsurprisingly, this method wasn't scalable (or entirely accurate) and so a 'data accuracy officer' was appointed by the Manchester Guardian Society in 1857.

Fast-forward to now, and the process is a lot more formalised, and a lot less Lady Whistledown. These days, your creditworthiness is based on a huge amount of data, not how friendly you are with the local candlestick maker.

Forever in your debt,

Lord Overdraft

could find it harder to borrow money, or have to pay higher interest. Lenders are taking a risk by lending you money, so they need to feel confident you can pay them back. But remember, your credit score's not the *only* thing lenders use to assess your eligibility. So try not to get too hung up on it. Instead, think of it as something you keep an eye on and nurture over time, giving it a little extra love in the lead-up to applying for credit.

Here are some ways to keep your credit score looking healthy:

- **Pay your bills on time, every time:** late or missed payments are a common way to damage your credit score. While on-time payments steadily build your credit history, even a single missed payment – especially one that's more than 30 days late – can be reported to credit bureaus and significantly lower your score. So it's best to set up direct debits or reminders to avoid slip-ups.

- **Check your credit report regularly:** you can view a basic version of your credit report online, for free. If you want a more detailed view, you'll usually have to pay a monthly subscription to one of the credit bureaus. Checking it regularly can help you spot mistakes that could negatively impact your score. If you spot something that doesn't look right, you can ask the credit bureaus to add something called a Notice of Correction, which is a note that explains what the problem is. This won't change your credit score, but it can give helpful context to lenders when they're checking your report. It is worth noting, though, that a lot of credit reports are read by automated systems, rather than lovely real-life humans. These automated systems don't always register nuanced updates like Notices of Correction, so might overlook them. If this happens, you should speak to your lender and ask them to re-review your report.

- **Stay on the electoral register:** make sure you're registered to vote at your current address. Aside from making you a good citizen, being on the electoral register gives lenders proof of your identity.

- **Build credit history:** your score might be low because you've never borrowed before or haven't lived in the UK for very long. You could consider using a credit card responsibly to get started. It can ding your score at first, but it helps show that you can borrow money and pay it back on time. Your score will always show as 'poor' if you never borrow money, even if you're a sensible spender.

- **Avoid maxing out credit:** a credit limit is a ceiling, not a target! Use less than 30% of your max if you can. Even if you pay on time, getting close to your limit every month can lower your score as it suggests you rely on borrowing.

Good debt versus bad debt

You've probably heard debt being described as *good* or *bad* before. You might naturally think of good debt as getting a mortgage for a house, and bad debt as putting designer cowboy boots on a credit card. But it's not the items *themselves* that define whether the debt's good or bad. It's to do with you and your personal situation – the comfort zone we talked about earlier.

Basically, *good debt* is debt that's manageable, fits in with your budget and helps fund something that adds value to your life. Like taking out a loan on a car you need to travel to work every day. *Bad debt* is the opposite. It's when you borrow money without being certain you can pay it back, like taking out a car loan on a whim, even though you're not sure you can afford it long term.

If you're not sure what camp your debt falls into, take a moment to ask yourself the questions on the following page.

Part 1: Taking on debt

Let's look at when and why you might borrow money . . .

- **To keep your cash flowing:** you borrow money to help keep your cash flow steady, so you don't have to drastically cut back when something unexpected happens or miss out when you spot a good deal on something you've been meaning to buy. That doesn't mean buying something you don't need just because it's on offer, like a brand new blender, when the blender you already have works just fine. Just that if you have an emergency, like spilling green juice all over your laptop, using a credit card or paying on finance lets you deal with the situation straight away, without spending your entire monthly budget upfront.

THE GOOD/BAD CAFE

5 Mint Way,
Sterling Vale, SV1 5RC,
United Kingdom

ITEM:	(YES)	(NO)	(MAYBE)
Is there another way to pay, like tweaking my budget or saving up?	☐	☐	☐
Am I sure I can pay the money back in time?	☐	☐	☐
Do I have a safety net in case something goes wrong?	☐	☐	☐
Will the thing I'm borrowing money for add value to my life or help me reach my goals?	☐	☐	☐
Do I fully understand all the terms, like possible penalties for late repayments?	☐	☐	☐
Have I shopped around for the best deal and compared different interest rates, fees and terms?	☐	☐	☐

Thank you! Come again!

- **To buy big-ticket items:** you need somewhere to live and a mode of transport *today*, not in 30 years' time. So things like houses and cars are big, upfront expenses that many people buy now and pay off over time.

  We cover mortgages in a lot of detail in chapter 10, but in simple terms a mortgage is a long-term loan that helps you buy a home by spreading the cost over a number of years. With most common mortgage types, repayments cover both the interest and the amount you borrowed. Early on, most of your repayments go towards the interest, but over time, more goes towards paying off the loan itself.

  You might have heard people say they're getting a car on finance, too. The most common way to do this is via a personal contract purchase (PCP) – a type of loan that lets you buy a car without paying the full amount upfront. Instead, you pay a deposit followed by monthly repayments. The cost of the monthly repayments is based on the length of the loan (the term), your deposit amount, and how flashy the car is. At the end of the term, you usually have the option to return the car, trade it in, or make a final payment to buy the car outright.

- **To pay for school:** studying or special training can be expensive. But it might make sense to borrow money to pay for it if it means you can earn more money later on. A common way to do this is by getting a student loan. The name is a little misleading as they're actually pretty different from most other types of loan. Unlike a mortgage or PCP, student loan repayments work more like a tax – how much you repay is based on how much you earn. And you only start repaying the loan once you earn over a certain amount of money, which varies depending on your plan type.

While interest does accrue on your balance, the amount you repay still depends on your income, not the balance itself. So unless you're earning way more

than the threshold, paying off a student loan early doesn't usually make sense. Plus, after a certain number of years, the loan is written off completely (when this happens depends on which student loan plan you're on). With all that in mind, you might want to think about prioritising other financial goals or high-interest debts and let your student loan repayments naturally adjust with your income.

Their debt is your debt

Like we said in the 'Doing money together' chapter, your finances become connected when you share your life with another person. The same applies to debt. For example, if you co-signed on a loan with a partner, you're both equally responsible for paying it back. And in the event of divorce or death, you might be legally required to cover the repayments on your own, on top of an already stressful situation. If it comes to that, a professional, like a credit counsellor, can help you explore your options and create a plan. Just bear in mind that it can appear on your credit report and impact your credit score. If you're not sure what to do, there are lots of organisations who'll give you confidential, impartial advice – we've listed some at the end of this chapter. You can also get legal advice from a solicitor.

The cost of borrowing

The fact is, borrowing money almost always costs money (there are exceptions, though, like credit cards if you pay them off in full and on time each month). The cost of borrowing depends on a few factors including . . .

1. **The interest rate:** this is the cost of borrowing the money – essentially, you're paying your lender a percentage of what you borrow. This is also where compound interest comes in, which we talked about in the 'Principles for your money' chapter. When you're saving it works in your favour, but when you owe money and aren't paying off your balance it could work against you. Depending on the type of credit you use, you could be racking up debt by paying interest *on your interest*, plus interest on any missed repayments. This means if you don't pay your debt off quickly, the items you bought will cost far more than their sticker price.

2. **Fees:** any extra charges, like an initial fee for setting up an account, or regular charges like an annual membership fee for a credit card.

3. **Time:** the longer you take to repay a loan, the more interest you pay. Spreading out your repayments might make big purchases feel more affordable, but it's important to find the balance between paying it off in a timeframe that suits you, and not paying too much interest for the privilege.

Because interest rates, fees and repayment periods differ so much from lender to lender, they use something known as

INTEREST RATE
10%

LOAN
AMOUNT
£1,200

MONTHLY
REPAYMENTS
£105

TOTAL
AMOUNT
TO REPAY
£1,263

TOTAL INTEREST
OWED OVER 12 MOS
£63

APR (or annual percentage rate) to make it easier to compare the cost of borrowing. The APR looks at how much it'd cost you to borrow money for one year, taking into account the interest rate and other fees. Lenders have to tell you the APR before you sign a credit agreement.

When it comes to paying back a loan, there are a few different ways you can do it. You might want to have a direct debit to come straight from your bank account. Automating payments like this is super convenient, as you can set it up and forget about it. If you can afford it, you may even have the option to pay off your loan faster by making extra payments, but check with your lender first as they sometimes apply extra costs. If you have multiple debts, you can sometimes consolidate them into one single loan – more on that at the end of this chapter.

Case study

'A loan helped me become my own boss.'

Coral, 41, is a beautician who lives on the outskirts of Bristol. Since her early 20s, she's worked for salons in the city but always hoped to start her own business.

The house she shares with her husband has a small garden room that they've never really used, so she decided to repurpose it as a salon. Once she checked she was allowed to use the space to run a business, she moved on to the fun part: decorating it. She had enough money saved to add aesthetic touches to the space, but needed a little extra to pay for a reclining treatment chair and manicure table. To help her get there, Coral decided to take out a personal loan for £1,200. She had a play around on a calculator to check out the different term options.

Here's a breakdown of the terms of an 18-month loan:

- **Loan amount:** £1,200
- **Interest rate:** 10%
- **Monthly repayments:** £71.83
- **Total interest owed over 18 months:** £93
- **Total amount to repay:** £1,293

And here's a breakdown of the terms of a 12-month loan:

- **Loan amount:** £1,200
- **Interest rate:** 10%
- **Monthly repayments:** £105.26
- **Total interest owed over 12 months:** £63
- **Total amount to repay:** £1,263

Even though the monthly repayments were lower with the 18-month loan, Coral would owe more interest because she was paying it back over a longer period of time. In the end, she decided she'd rather take the 12-month term. It worked out cheaper, and she wouldn't have a loan hanging over her for as long.

To make sure this fitted with her monthly budget, Coral did some forecasting. She predicted that she'd see around

25 customers a week, with the average appointment costing £28. This made her forecasted monthly take-home pay around £2,300. Using this as a guide, Coral felt confident that the 12-month loan repayments would fit within her monthly budget.

Dealing with debt

Even if you plan to stay on top of your debt repayments, sometimes life can get complicated. And things can spiral very quickly. A few missed payments can mean you're stung by extra fees and added interest, and negatively impact your credit score. Dealing with the situation can suddenly become very expensive and stressful.

Realising that your debt is getting out of control can feel crushing, affecting everything from your sleep to your mood, and even your relationships. What's worse is that feelings of shame and guilt often make people want to hide from the problem, delaying action and making things even harder. If you feel this way, you're far from alone: almost 50% of people feel anxious about keeping up with their credit commitments.[1]

Acting sooner rather than later can lift a huge weight off your shoulders if you're in a situation where you've started to fall behind on bills or debt repayments. Taking these small steps straight away can make a big difference:

- **Share with someone you trust:** a friend, family member or financial adviser can help you to gain some perspective. We've also listed some free debt advice services towards the end of this chapter. Don't feel like you have to keep this situation a secret – remember, struggling with debt is more common than you think.

- **Limit any new debt:** take your credit cards off preset checkouts and out of your Apple Pay or Google Pay. This'll stop you from making any accidental or unconscious purchases and force you to pause before you click 'pay'.

- **Remember the 50–30–20 rule from chapter 4:** rethink your overall budget to make space for debt repayments. This might mean temporarily reducing (or even removing) the amount you're putting into savings or allocating some of your 'needs' to debt repayment.

Watch out for your own red-flag behaviours

Sometimes debt can creep up on you, getting out of control before you even realise. So try to be self-aware and look out for behaviours that might indicate you're headed for trouble before things get out of hand. Here are a few examples to watch out for . . .

- **Using different buy now, pay later (BNPL) services:** yep, that interest-free, pay-in-three service is a form of credit. Using BNPL at checkout can be a useful way to make expensive purchases feel more manageable.

But it's important that you're using these services responsibly – paying them back on time, and in full – and not as a way to splurge on something you can't actually afford. If you notice that you're tapping this option every time you proceed to checkout, this could be a sign that you're spending impulsively. These services usually charge late payment fees, which can add up fast if you're not on top of your repayments. Plus, late payments can be reported to credit bureaus and damage your credit score.

- **Only making the minimum repayments:** only paying off the minimum balance makes your debt more expensive in the long run, since it'll take you longer to clear it. If you're doing this, it's probably a sign that you're struggling to pay for the debt you took on.

- **Maxing out your credit limit:** if you're doing this every month, that could mean your spend is creeping up.

- **Using your overdraft as a 'loan':** you go into your overdraft any time you spend more money than you have in your account. It can be useful in the short term or to help with unexpected costs, but using it to consistently spend beyond your means could be a red flag. You usually have to pay your overdraft back with added interest, so relying on it can mean you're racking up more debt. Plus, unlike a loan or credit card, there isn't usually an obligation to pay it off each month, so it's easy for an overdraft to escalate.

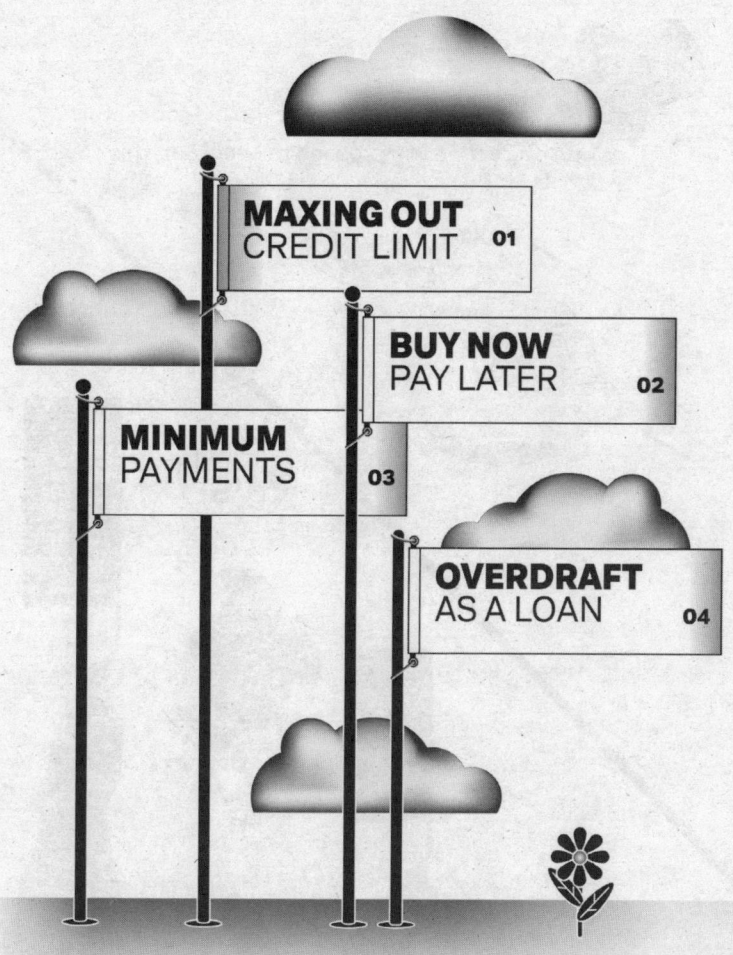

MAXING OUT
CREDIT LIMIT   01

BUY NOW
PAY LATER   02

MINIMUM
PAYMENTS   03

OVERDRAFT
AS A LOAN   04

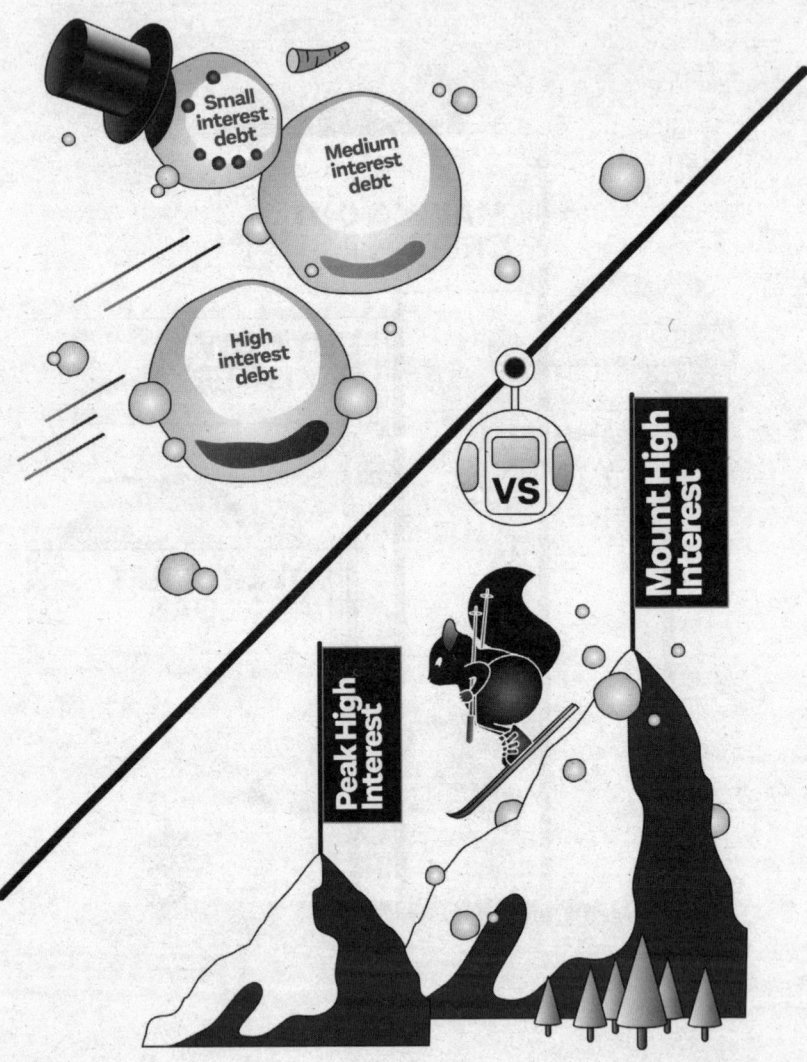

Methods for paying off debt

If you're losing grip of your debt and feeling a bit out in the cold (financially speaking), there are two main debt repayment strategies you could try: the *snowball* and the *avalanche*.

With the snowball method, you start by clearing the smallest debt, alongside making minimum repayments on remaining debt you have elsewhere. Once you've paid off the smallest debt, close the account, and then move on to the next smallest. While paying off the minimum balance makes your debt more expensive in the long run, this approach can help keep you motivated. Watching yourself rack up the little wins will keep you pushing forward.

With the avalanche method, you pay off the debt with the highest interest rate first, costing you less in interest over time. Once that's paid, you move on to the one with the next highest rate. When it comes to picking a method, it's all about choosing the one that works best for you and keeps you motivated! Some people prefer quicker wins, some like to know they're saving money in the long run, and almost everyone hates icy conditions. Just remember to wrap up warm, no matter which you choose.

Debt consolidation

Debt consolidation is another way to tackle debt that feels unmanageable. It's when you combine multiple debts into one single loan, typically with a lower interest rate and longer term, to simplify what you owe and bring down your monthly expenses. This is especially helpful if you're managing high-interest credit card debt, store cards or personal loans, as it can lower the total interest you pay and streamline everything into one predictable payment. If you're not sure this is quite right for you, the organisations we've listed at the end of this chapter can talk you through your options.

There are three main ways you can consolidate your debt.

- **Personal loans:** you might qualify for a fixed-rate loan to cover your debts, which you then pay off over a set period. A fixed interest rate and consistent monthly repayments will give you clarity and control, but getting approved for one will still depend on your credit score and having a reliable source of income.

- **Balance transfer credit cards:** for credit card debt, balance transfer cards offer a period (usually 12–24 months) of 0% interest. There's usually a 1–5% fee for this type of card, but this is often lower than the interest you'd pay on your old cards, so you'd still be saving money in the long run. Just be sure to pay off the balance before the initial interest-free period ends to avoid interest kicking in.

- **Debt consolidation loans:** these are designed specifically to cover high-interest debts and can help spread repayments over a manageable timeline. Approval, interest rates and terms vary, so shop around for the best rate. Consolidation can improve your cash flow and reduce your stress – even if your debt is still manageable – but it's really important to make sure that the repayment plan fits into your budget, and always consider fees and penalties.

Getting help repaying debt

If you've tried some of these methods but you still need help, you can look into repayment plans. These are agreements lenders sometimes offer to make debt repayments more affordable. If you need some guidance on setting one up, the organisations we've listed at the end of this chapter can help, or you can reach out to your bank or lender. While these plans can be really useful, just bear in mind that they can show up on your credit report and impact your credit score.

- **Debt management plans** (DMPs) are a formal agreement between you and your creditors (like a credit card company) to pay off your debt over time – usually a number of years, but it depends how much debt you're in. Often, a third party, like a charity, arranges one for you. These show up on your credit report and could impact it negatively, making it harder to get credit and more likely you'll have to pay a higher interest rate. That said, if you keep up with the repayments, having a DMP on your report usually looks better than having unpaid debts.

- **Temporary repayment plans** are a more informal solution you arrange directly with your creditor, where you temporarily reduce or skip repayments altogether. This option might be a better fit if you just need some temporary relief, like if you have to take a period of unpaid time off work. These can also show up on your credit report and impact it in similar ways to a debt management plan.

Paying off debt is a great achievement. And it also presents a great opportunity – a clever way to trick yourself into saving money. It's called the 'debt to savings hack'. Think of it like this: you've been paying off your debt over a period of time, meaning you're already in the habit of putting aside a specific amount of money each month. So once you've paid off your debt, you could continue putting that same amount into savings without even feeling it.

Case study

'I got myself into nearly £2,000 worth of debt by helping a family member.'

Joe, 27, is a chef at a trendy restaurant in Manchester. He rents a flat in the city with one flatmate. Joe can be a bit impulsive but generally thinks of himself as being OK with money. He sticks to a rough budget and even managed to build up £925 in savings over a year.

One day, his cousin Oli called him. He was stressed because he'd lost his job and couldn't pay his rent that month. Straight away, Joe offered to cover Oli's rent. Using up his savings to help his cousin out was a little scary, but he was sure Oli would pay him back as soon as he found a new job. He didn't want to ask when that would be, in case it made Oli even more anxious.

A few weeks later, Joe and his girlfriend split up (he insists it was mutual). Even though he knew it was for the best, Joe was a bit down about the whole thing, so he decided to treat himself a little. Since his savings were wiped out, Joe used a couple of buy now, pay later options at checkout and got himself a credit card. He bought himself a record player, some trainers and a new tattoo (to cover up the matching one he got with his ex). It was all a great distraction. Joe knew he'd been spending more than usual, but he pushed it to the back of his mind. When he finally came to look at his bank account, he felt sick. He owed £20 in missed payment fees on the BNPL sites, plus £1,830 on the credit card, and the interest was adding up.

Joe reassured himself that some of this would be sorted out when Oli paid him back. He texted him and asked for the money, but Oli said he didn't know when he'd be able to repay him. At this point, Joe started to panic; he'd banked on that money to help get him out of debt. Joe needed someone to talk to, so he called a friend and confided in him. His friend calmed him down and suggested Joe speak to Oli about setting up a repayment plan. It was an awkward conversation but Oli agreed he'd pay Joe back £200 a month for the next four months.

That sorted a big chunk of his debt, but there was interest piling up on the rest. Joe's trusty friend suggested he could move the debt to a balance transfer credit card that wouldn't charge him interest for 12 months. He looked at his budget and worked out how much he could afford to pay back every month, then set up a direct debit on payday that went straight to paying it off. He was debt-free in seven months, and over his break-up in eight.

Handy resources

If you're in need of help that's free, confidential and impartial, all of these organisations can support you.

- **StepChange:** a debt charity that'll listen to your worries and help you create an actionable plan. You can reach them online, by phone (0800 138 1111) or by post.

- **Citizens Advice:** a charity that provides advice on debt, money management, housing, employment and benefits. You can reach them online or by phone (0800 144 8848, or 0800 702 2020 if you're based in Wales).

- **MoneyHelper:** a service that provides money guidance and debt advice. You can reach them online or by phone (0800 138 7777, or 0800 138 0555 if you're in Wales).

- **National Debtline:** an independent debt advice charity. You can reach them online or by phone (0808 808 4000).

- **PayPlan:** a debt advice service that offers solutions like debt management plans and help with bankruptcy. You can reach them online or by phone (0800 316 1833).

- **Turn2Us:** a national charity providing help to people who are struggling financially. You can reach them online.

- **Entitledto:** an organisation that helps people work out which benefits they can claim from national and local governments. You can reach them online.

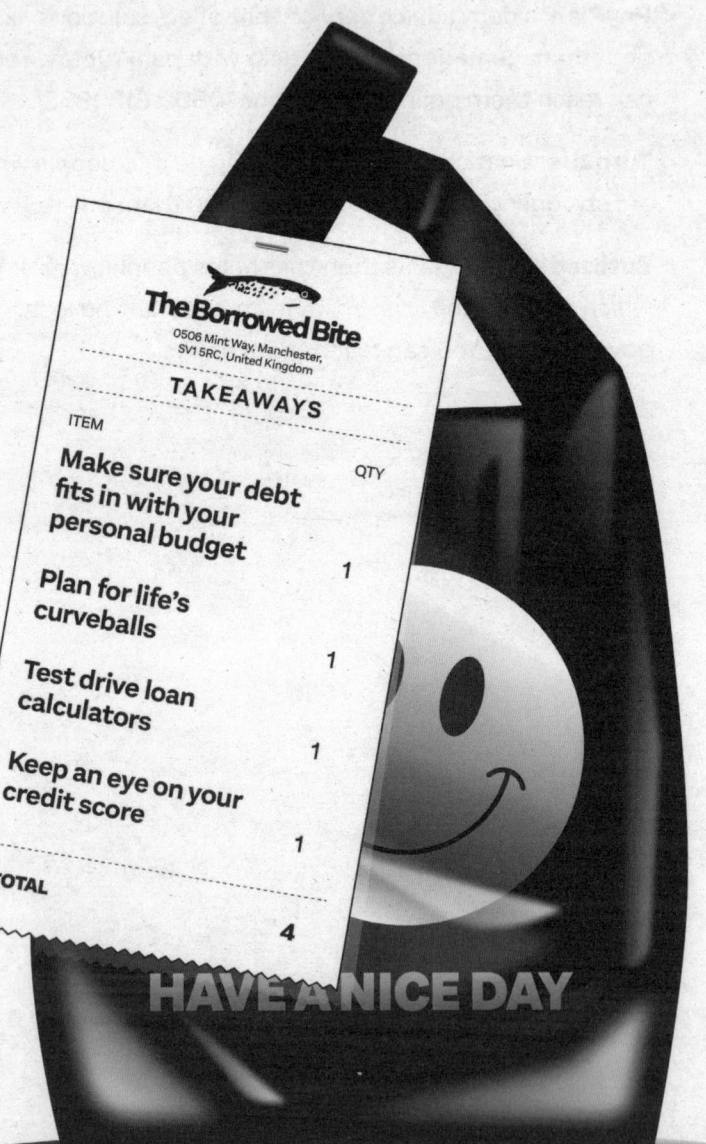

The Borrowed Bite

0506 Mint Way, Manchester,
SV1 5RC, United Kingdom

TAKEAWAYS

ITEM	QTY
Make sure your debt fits in with your personal budget	1
Plan for life's curveballs	1
Test drive loan calculators	1
Keep an eye on your credit score	1
TOTAL	4

HAVE A NICE DAY

TAKEAWAYS

Make sure your debt fits in with your personal budget: and aligns with your goals and priorities. Don't stretch yourself beyond your means – know your limits and capabilities.

Plan for life's curveballs: ask yourself whether you could still make repayments if you hit an unexpected snag, like you suddenly had to pay out for a vet bill. Have a back-up plan (a safety net, insurance or a rich uncle) just in case.

Test drive loan calculators: play around with loan calculators to see how different amounts and timeframes change your repayment. Remember that the longer the repayment period, the more interest you'll pay, increasing the total cost of your loan. And don't forget to watch out for hidden fees.

Keep an eye on your credit score: while your credit score isn't the be-all and end-all, it *does* give you a good sense of how lenders see you, and can either help or hurt you when the time comes to apply for a loan or credit. Try to see it as a long-term thing that you watch and nurture over time.

Chapter 7
Strategies for saving

They're diligent, they're nimble and they have fabulous tails – but most importantly, squirrels are nature's ultimate super savers. It's what they're built for. The phrase 'squirrelling away' literally means to save or stash something valuable. But here's a fun fact: squirrels lose track of up to 75% of the nuts they hide![1] That's right, saving can be tough, even for the pros.

Luckily, most of us aren't burying our money under the nearest tree and hoping for the best. Around 68% of people have a savings account,[2] and 61% of adults save money either every month or most months. But even though we know it's important, it can be hard to make room for savings in a budget that already feels stretched. It's not surprising that a third of people said they wouldn't have enough to live off for more than a month, when the cost of living is high and essentials are more expensive than ever. Plus, spending makes us feel good in the moment; it's immediately gratifying and exciting. Saving, on the other hand, can be easy to put off. But as we've said before, and will *definitely* say again, the goal should always be to pay yourself first.

Why? Because saving represents freedom. Savings are your lifeline when your washing machine breaks down, or your key to unlocking that dream holiday. It's the deposit for your first home and the ability to enjoy life when you retire. Saving – wherever and whenever you can – is something positive you can do for yourself.

How much should I be saving?

You'll have a clearer idea of what you can afford to save once you've balanced your budget (check out chapter 4). Generally, aiming to save 20% of your income is a good target to shoot for, based on the popular 50–30–20 rule. In this model, 50% goes towards *needs* (housing, bills), 30% to *wants* (socialising, hobbies) and 20% towards *savings, investments* and *debt repayment*. But it's important to do what works for you. If 20% is out of reach, don't panic! Something is better than nothing. Even saving a small amount each month is a win.

In our 'Principles for your money' chapter, we talked about setting goals, which is key here. Whether you're saving for a coffee machine, a home deposit, or just to feel more secure about your finances in general, having a clear goal gives you a target and helps you figure out the best saving strategy for getting there. Almost half of all Monzo Pots created in the last 12 months had a goal attached to them, and our most popular Pot names probably won't surprise you at all – check them out on the next page.

Start with an emergency fund, known as a *safety net*. This is a stash of money you set aside specifically for unexpected events, from illness to a broken boiler. (We talk about this in more detail in the 'Balancing your budget' chapter.) Most people aim for three to six months' worth of living expenses, giving you breathing room to handle what life throws at you.

What are interest rates all about?

Before we go any further, let's talk about interest as it'll crop up a lot in this chapter. *Interest* is a percentage that a bank either adds to your savings or charges you on a loan. So in the case of saving, interest is a good thing!

The interest *rate* refers to the actual percentage. For example, if you save £100 in an account with a 2% interest rate (more on savings accounts soon), after one year you'll have £102. The higher the rate, the more your savings will grow, so it's worth shopping around for the best deal. In the UK, these rates are influenced by the Bank of England, which sets what's known as the 'base rate'. This is the benchmark that banks and lenders use to set their own interest rates. The Bank of England sometimes changes the base rate to help control inflation and stabilise the economy. When this happens, it has a knock-on effect on the interest rates that banks and lenders offer.

Where should I put my savings?

The clue is in the name – one sensible place to put your savings is in a savings account. This keeps savings separate from the money in your current account (so you don't accidentally spend your holiday money on household bills, or vice versa) but also has additional benefits, mainly related to the amount of interest you can earn, depending on how long you keep your money in there.

There are a few types of savings accounts. Let's take a look at the differences between them.

Easy access savings accounts

Easy access by name, easy access by nature. You can usually take your cash out whenever you like, and you don't have to pay a penalty fee for withdrawing your money like you do with some other types of savings accounts. They typically offer lower interest rates than the account types listed below, but if you're just getting started, saving for a short-term goal, or need immediate access to your funds, this is a great first step.

Regular savings accounts

Great for people who plan to save smaller amounts regularly rather than stashing away a big chunk all at once. Regular savings accounts might give you better interest rates than their easy access cousins, but there are usually some extra terms to follow – you might need to commit to paying a certain amount of money each month, and missing a deposit could mean losing out on that sweet, sweet interest.

Notice savings accounts

This is one for the planners. With a notice savings account, you'll have to give advance notice – anywhere from 30 to 180 days – before withdrawing your money, and there are usually limitations on how much you can take out in one calendar year. It's great if you want to benefit from higher interest rates and don't need instant access to your cash.

Fixed-rate savings accounts

If you've got a lump sum you're definitely not going to need anytime soon, a fixed-rate account could be just the ticket. You lock your money away for a set period – usually between six months and five years – and in return you get a guaranteed interest rate. (But remember, that also means the interest rate won't increase – or decrease! – in line with the Bank of England base rate.) Think of it like a financial slow cooker: set it and forget it, and enjoy a tasty return at the end. Just remember, these accounts are for the long haul, so they're best suited for money you won't need in a pinch.

There's no need to pick just one type of savings account. You might want to put your money in a few different places as you move through life's stages. When you're just starting out and you're focused on saving for shorter-term goals, like creating your safety net, you'll probably find that an easy access account does the job. But as you get older, you might shift your focus to longer-term goals, like buying a home or building up your savings, making fixed-rate accounts more appealing, alongside other savings and investments.

What about an ISA?

If a savings account is a gift, an ISA (which stands for Individual Savings Account) is a type of wrapping paper that shields the account from tax. When you earn interest on a savings account, it counts towards your taxable income (although the

interest in a savings account might still be free from tax if the amount is below your personal savings allowance).

Each tax year (6 April to 5 April) you can save or invest up to £20,000, across as many different ISA accounts as you like. But the rules around ISAs could change, and they've actually been debated by policymakers recently! Always check the government website for the latest. As long as you don't exceed the annual deposit allowance, the interest you earn in an ISA is tax-free. This amount doesn't roll over, so you have to use it or lose it. There are ISA versions of most types of savings accounts that come with many of the same benefits and limitations (except the interest is tax-free!). Not everyone will be eligible for an ISA, so make sure you check the government website for the specifics.

Whatever account you choose, don't forget: the Financial Services Compensation Scheme (FSCS) protects your eligible savings up to £85,000 if your bank, building society or credit union goes out of business.

Money challenges

Turning saving into a game can make a big difference to whether you stick with it. Here are some of our customers' favourite challenges:

- **The 1p savings challenge:** this challenge starts small and builds up over time. On day one, you move a humble 1p into your savings account, on day two, you add 2p, and so on. On the final day of the year you'll be saving only

£3.65 for a grand total of . . . wait for it . . . £667.95. It's
effective because it seems easy, yet you can save a solid
chunk of change without even noticing. Not impressed
yet? Make it multiples of 10p and you'll end your year with
£6,679.50 instead. Imagine what you could do with that!

If you don't want to commit to doing this every day,
start with £1 in week one, £2 in week two, and by week 52
you're saving £52 and end up with a whopping £1,378 in
your savings pot. This is a good option if you find it easier
to save more as the year goes on. If the opposite is true,
and you know the end of the year is going to be more of a
struggle, you can reverse the challenge – start with £52
in week one, and decrease from there, until you add that
final, triumphant £1 in the last week of December.

There are apps that automate these challenges for
you, or you can go old-school with a printed chart and a
piggy bank, and tick off each day as you go. In 2025, over a
million Monzo customers tried a version of this challenge.

- **The monthly savings challenge:** this one works on a
  month-by-month basis, making it a good option for
  setting aside holiday money. You start in January by
  saving £10, then £20 in February, £30 in March and so
  on until December, when you save £120. By the end of
  the year, you'll have saved £780 – enough for a weekend
  away and a suitcase full of swimming pool inflatables
  you definitely shouldn't have brought home and will
  never use again.

- **The save your age challenge:** a simple but effective challenge that the whole family can get in on. Each month, you each save the number of pounds in your age – if you're five you save £5, if you're 55 then . . . well, you get it.

- **The save for a rainy day challenge:** every cloud has a silver lining, and never more so than with this challenge, where you put away £5 every day it rains. Just don't tell your friend you're praying for a downpour on their wedding day so you can hit your savings target. You can do this challenge with anything that happens randomly or occasionally. Like putting aside a fiver every time we tell you to visit the government website in this book.

Saving doesn't have to be a chore. By turning it into a game and introducing a little bit of competition with family and friends, it can become something you actually enjoy.

Round-ups

If you're not someone who loves a challenge, why not take the lazy route instead? This savings strategy is so easy you might not even notice it's happening. It works like this: every time you spend, you round up your purchase to the nearest pound and save the difference. Bought a coffee for £2.40? Round it up to £3 and stash the extra 60p. If you're using cash, a coin wallet or piggy bank will work perfectly – just drop your small change straight in. If you're using a debit card, it's even easier as there are banking apps that'll do it for you. You'll be amazed at how quickly the pennies add up! Almost 1 in 5 of our customers use the round-up strategy, and it helps them save an average of £131 extra a year.[3]

Case study

'I created a safety net by saving the pennies.'

Laurie, 40, is a delivery driver from Liverpool. He's also Mo Salah's biggest fan, but that's not really relevant right now.

As a self-employed worker with fluctuating hours, Laurie always found it difficult to save money.

One day, he got a flat tyre. He needed to get it repaired urgently so he could carry on working, but he didn't have any savings behind him. Laurie knew he'd have to ask his sister if he could borrow the cash from her. He felt a bit awkward, but he couldn't think of any other option.

This scenario gave Laurie the push he needed to finally create himself a safety net. But he knew he'd need to find a savings method that felt as effortless as possible, otherwise he wouldn't stick to it. Laurie already used a banking app as a way to split bills with his friends when they went out. He decided to check out some of the other features and discovered there were clever ways to automate his savings, like rounding up his purchases to the nearest pound. He switched the round-up feature on and sent the spare change to a savings pot. He also set himself a challenge to put aside £10 every week. He always did it on a Monday morning as a way to kick off his week and make it part of his routine.

After one year, Laurie was shocked at how much he'd been able to save this way.

Here's what he found:

- **Small change makes a big impact:** small amounts really can add up to significant savings over time. From saving a small amount each week and turning on round-ups, Laurie saved nearly £650 in 12 months.
- **Automating = effortless:** Laurie loved that he didn't even have to *think* about saving. By automating round-ups on his banking app, it felt effortless – he didn't even notice he was doing it.
- **A safety net creates comfort:** just knowing that he had a pot to use in a pinch had such a positive impact on his mental health, and meant he didn't feel as panicked about unexpected costs.

Once Laurie saw how much of a difference saving made, he decided to make a habit of it. He kept his automated round-ups on and once the football season kicked off he started a new challenge – putting a pound aside every time Liverpool scored a goal, and a tenner when they won.

Saving is like any other life skill; the more you do it, the better you get at it. And there are plenty of ways to make it easier. Automating your savings is a game-changer. Set it up once, and you won't even have to think about it. Or turn savings into something fun with a challenge. It's just like Super Mario, except the prizes are real. The most important thing is keeping sight of your goals. This sets an intention for your money and makes the act of saving feel even more meaningful. Remembering this makes saving less of a chore, and more of a stepping stone to the life you want.

Save & Savor Bistro

0606 Capital Close, Manchester,
SV1 5RC, United Kingdom

TAKEAWAYS

ITEM	QTY
Pay yourself first	1
Start small	1
Shop around	1
Enjoy it	1
TOTAL	4

HAVE A NICE DAY

TAKEAWAYS

Pay yourself first: we're going to keep saying it – set aside savings as soon as you get paid. Better yet, automate it.

Start small: tiny amounts add up, so start saving whatever you can. Remember, even something small, like spare change from daily round-ups, can grow into something meaningful, like a safety net.

Shop around: compare savings accounts to get the best interest rates and terms for your money. And when you feel more confident, try setting up different types of accounts to suit your different goals.

Enjoy it: saving isn't about hoarding money away, never to touch it again – you saved it for a *reason*. So when you hit your goal, enjoy the feeling of spending your money on whatever it is you saved it for. You've done the hard work, so make sure you reap the rewards!

Just put £80 in an ISA and suddenly it's like I'm the Wolf of Wall Street, only much better looking.

Chapter 8
Becoming an investor

Remember when we said squirrels forget about 75% of the nuts they stash? They may have a reputation as nature's most adorable savers, but they might actually be her best investors too. Stashing nuts for one winter is smart, but burying them and forgetting they exist for a few winters is even smarter. Why settle for a handful of nuts now when you could grow yourself a tree and create a lifetime supply? It's a risk, but it might pay off.

And that, in a nutshell, is what investing is all about. Sacrificing a little bit now in the hope you'll get more back later. It sounds enticing, so why doesn't everyone do it? The world of investments can feel like a confusing mess of big promises and small print, which is enough to put people off ever trying. And while Brits may be fairly confident savers, they're much more cautious about investing.[1] To many, it might feel like something only the super rich or super savvy can do. When you think of an investor you might picture a gilet-clad man working in finance, but what if we told you that in the UK, Gen Z invests more than any previous generation? Over half of UK adults (51%) have invested in *something* as of 2024, which is about 27 million people![2] And it's up from 42% in 2023, which means the number of investors in the UK is growing really quickly, especially among young people.[3] Even though we're dipping a toe in the pool, we're still much more reluctant and cautious about it than in other places, like the United States.[4] By its very nature, investing involves a degree of uncertainty, which can make people feel nervous. If you stash your money under a mattress or in a savings account, you can be reasonably confident it'll stay where you left it. But when you invest, you put your money into something, like shares in a company. Those things can go up or down in value over time, and there's always a risk you could lose everything you put in.

There are a couple of myths around what a typical investor looks like that we'll bust before we even get into the specifics.

The first is that you need lots of money to start investing. It may have been true for previous generations, when investing was limited to stockbrokers in the corridors of exclusive banks, but the last 15 or so years have seen it become much more accessible. Now, anyone can invest online, starting with as little as a pound.

The second myth is that you need to be a seasoned professional with some kind of secret access to the world of investing. You do need to understand what you're investing in and the risk you're taking on, but you don't have to have a wealth of super specialised knowledge to get started with some ready-made options. When it comes to the things you can invest in, there are literally endless possibilities, from funds to rare Pokémon cards to cryptocurrencies. This chapter will focus on the options that are popular among beginners, and the key concepts that underpin investing.

Am I ready to be an investor?

Everyone can work towards investing, but it's a good idea to make sure you're in the right place financially first. Generally speaking, before you start investing you should prioritise:

- Paying off high-interest and short-term debts (like a credit card that's charging interest).
- Building a safety net of savings that would cover three to six months of living expenses for you and any dependents.
- Contributing to your pension regularly.

Investing works best when you treat it as a longer-term, steady practice, so a good rule of thumb is to invest money you won't need urgently in the next five years. If you do invest money you think you'll need soon, you might end up forced to sell at a bad time, without giving your investment time to mature and grow.

It's also really important you take the time to research any investment and feel confident you understand all the fine print (we'll get into what you should watch out for in this chapter). Each type of investment will carry its own risk and terms, and understanding these is essential.

And just because you start investing doesn't mean you

should stop putting money into savings. Investment returns aren't guaranteed, and although inflation can chip away at the value of your long-term savings, it's a good idea to have some easy-access money put away in case you need it. As in life, a varied diet is the healthiest choice.

What even *is* investing?

Investing is a label for a lot of different things, but broadly, it means you're putting your money into something that you hope will go up in value, but then again might not. You can invest in lots of things, from government bonds to Bitcoin and Birkin bags. If the value of those things rises or falls over time, investors stand to make or lose money on them.

Weathering the highs and lows of investing

Let's wind back the clock and pretend you invested in an ice cream van business 10 years ago. The value of your investment might have gone up if the ice cream business did well, like when it released a new flavour that went viral, or down when frozen yoghurt had us all in a chokehold. It might have peaked again in 2021, when we had four glorious weeks of sunshine, and got worse in 2024, when it was hot chocolate weather from June to September. Although it might have dipped a few times over the years, on the whole the business is doing well and even expanding to more vans in new locations. So it will have served you well to stay invested because the longer you invest, the more chance your money has to recover and beat those weather and frozen yoghurt-induced dips! How often an investment rises and falls is what's known as volatility – more on that later.

Investing isn't trading

That gilet-clad banker in a skyscraper you might instantly picture when you hear 'investor'? They're actually a professional trader, which means they buy and sell based on second-by-second price changes (or they're just a person who likes to layer). Some people do choose to trade individual stocks or bonds themselves, rather than relying on a professional trader to do it for them, but it's a time-consuming and risky strategy. This type of 'trading' involves reacting to market movements often (even daily) and it works best for people with a really good understanding of financial markets and risk.

The good news is you don't need to hunch over a screen tracking market movements to benefit from investing! Nowadays, there are plenty of options out there for first-time investors.

'The market'

The market may be where you buy tomatoes and fresh flowers, but it's also a common shorthand for the stock market. That's where people buy and sell shares in public companies on one of the many stock exchanges that exist around the world. The price of a company's shares changes all the time based on supply (how many existing investors want to sell them) and demand (how many people want to buy them). They'll make that decision based on how well a company's doing, the economy, and lots of other reasons. Every investor buys and sells shares for their own reasons, and it's this dynamic that keeps the market in a state of constant movement. There are other types of markets, too – for example, commodities markets, where people trade in raw materials like gold, coffee and chocolate.

Why invest?

Picture the scene. The year is 2001, and hot pink flip phones are all the rage. You're on your way to see a new film called *Shrek* and you stop at a corner shop to buy yourself a 10p Freddo to sneak into the cinema. You decide to get a scratch-card on a whim at the till and – result! You've just won yourself £100. It's shaping up to be a pretty spectacular day. As you're chewing on your Freddo and the trailers play, your mind starts to wander. What will you do with your new found fortune? Just as the sound of 'All Star' by Smash Mouth fills the cinema, you narrow it down to three options:

1. Put it in a savings account
2. Buy and eat 1,000 more Freddos
3. Invest it

Now if that really was you, and you really were lucky enough to have lived through the golden age of cinema and technology, what would you have chosen? If you'd bought a thousand Freddos in one go, you would have gained one great story (and possibly a stomach ache, depending on how quickly you ate them all).

If you'd put the money in a savings account, it would have earned roughly 2% in interest,[5] and you would have about £160 today, thanks to compounding. Not too shabby. Except that £160 wouldn't be worth as much today because of inflation – which is when the price of things goes up over time, meaning the same amount of money can buy you less (we talk about inflation in chapter 2). Your £160 could buy only 250 Freddos now, versus 1,000 with £100 back then, because the price of a Freddo has gone up from 10p to 40p.[6] So even though you've made a gain on your original £100, you're still on the back foot because of inflation.[7]

Let's imagine you had invested that £100 in a fund that tracks the biggest companies in the US, in an index called the S&P 500. At the end of 2024, that £100 would have been worth £789.54.[8] If you didn't touch your investment for 23 years, you'd see a potential growth of 8.52% per year, on average.[9] You'd need to adjust that growth for inflation,[10] which means you'd end up with an annual return of 5.15%. That's still higher than the savings rate of 2% and means your investment would actually beat inflation!

Aside from the fact that *Shrek* is timeless, there's another big takeaway to this story. When you set your money aside in savings, it might earn a small percentage of interest, but it's less likely to earn enough to outpace inflation. By investing some of your money, you're giving it a chance to grow faster than inflation. But inflation-beating growth isn't guaranteed. There's always a chance investments can go down in value or you could lose money, especially if you invest in riskier options like crypto. That's why it really pays to understand the risk you're taking on – more on that next.

Key investment concepts

If you're ready to take the plunge (or you've already started and want to learn more), we'll get into the specifics of *how* to actually invest in a moment. But before we do, it's really helpful to understand the following key factors that are within your control as an investor, like your risk appetite and timeline. That's because understanding them will help you manage the things you can't control, like an unsettled market, with a lot more confidence.

1. Risk

In the context of investing, risk appetite has nothing to do with your willingness to eat questionable street food. It's actually all about your attitude towards *risk* and *return*. *Risk* refers to the likelihood of losing what you invested, and *return* is what you stand to make on top of your original investment if it goes up in value. That's fundamentally differ-ent to savings, where the bank guarantees to give you back what you put in plus interest, if you've put your savings in an interest-bearing account. Sometimes you may see a visual risk score on a sliding scale going from least to most risky.

Figuring out how much risk you're willing and able to take on is a personal decision. But it might help to ask yourself if you care more about keeping your investment safe, even if it doesn't grow as much, or if you'd rather go for the highest

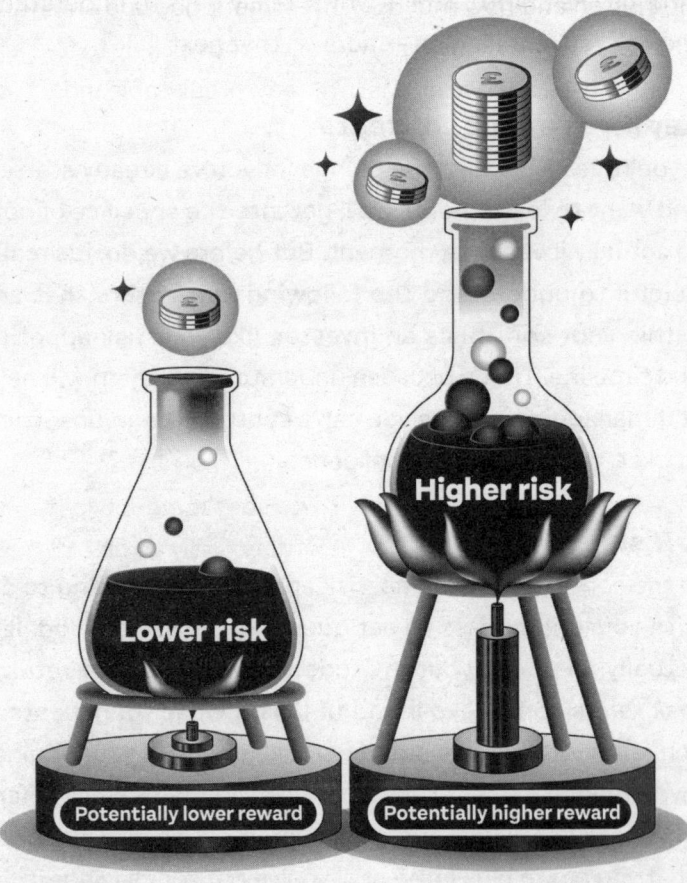

possible gain, even if there's risk involved. Based on your goals and how long you plan to stay invested, it's up to you to decide how much risk you're willing to take on – that's your 'risk appetite'.

2. Volatility

How often and how much an investment goes up and down in value is what's known as 'volatility'. You're likely to find less volatile investment options in steady, predictable industries like food or textiles, and markets like the UK, US or Singapore. More volatile investments are likely to come from more uncertain sectors or markets, and you'll see an example of that later on in this chapter when we get into cryptocurrency. A more volatile investment might be a riskier choice, especially if you choose to invest in it over a shorter period of time.

3. Diversifying

Also known as not putting all your eggs in one basket. Investing your money in lots of different things is a good idea, so if one of them doesn't do well, it's more likely to be balanced out by the success of others. Remember that ice cream van business we talked about? If you'd invested in that, plus a hot chocolate stand and a yoga studio, for good measure, you'd have been less reliant on just one of those things doing well. Putting your money into a variety of investments over a long period of time means you're spreading out the risk you're taking on. Plenty of investment options, like funds, pick a variety of investments for you for exactly this reason.

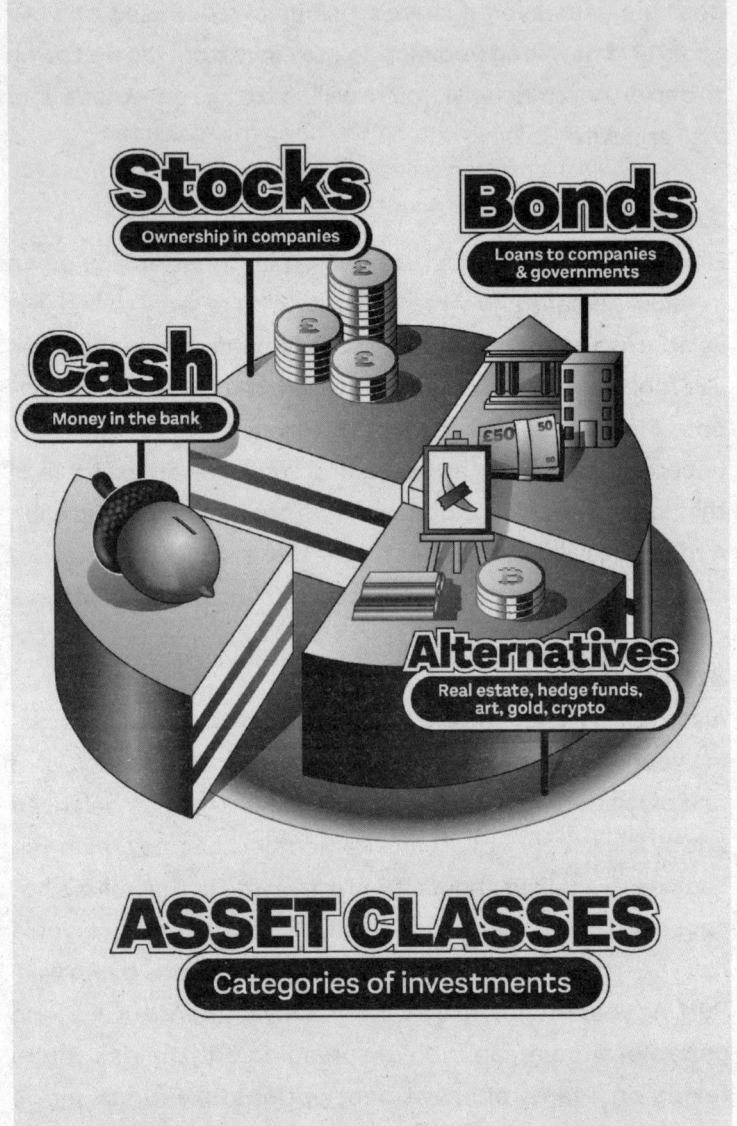

Stocks
Ownership in companies

Bonds
Loans to companies & governments

Cash
Money in the bank

Alternatives
Real estate, hedge funds, art, gold, crypto

ASSET CLASSES
Categories of investments

Shares, bonds and other assets

There are lots of different types of investment you can make, which are often called 'asset classes'. Putting your money into a range of them helps diversify your 'portfolio', which is a fancy word people use to describe the collection of things you invest in.

Stocks and shares: shares are units of ownership in a company sold on a stock exchange. You can make money when you buy lower than you sell, or when a company pays out dividends. Some companies pay their shareholders dividends if they make a profit and choose to give some of it back to shareholders, either as a one-off or regular payment. You'll find different companies have different levels of risk attached to them, like any other investment. A hot new AI company that's only been around six months is usually riskier than a utility company that's been going for decades and shown steady growth.

Bonds: governments and companies need to borrow money just like people do, and that's essentially what bonds are. When you buy a bond, you're lending your money to a company or government for a set period of time, at a set interest rate. A bond's equivalent of dividends are coupons – payouts throughout the year that represent interest. Then at a fixed time, when the bond reaches 'maturity', investors make a return. At a really basic level, bonds are thought of as pretty steady investments. They're less likely to massively tank in value, but the flipside is that they're not going to suddenly soar either. Bear in mind that if you invest in government bonds in politically unpredictable countries, or companies without a solid track record, there's a bigger risk attached. Bonds have risk ratings – from AAA (lower risk) down to C and even D (higher risk).

Cash: we talked about cash in the 'Strategies for saving' chapter (and in every other chapter and page of this book). That's when you put money into a savings account and earn interest on your deposits. Earning interest on interest, when you leave savings be, is a low-risk way to let that sweet, sweet compound interest build up.

Alternatives: this covers almost everything else! Handbags. Cryptocurrencies. Art. Gold. A tissue a celebrity once sneezed into. Almost anything we humans have assigned value to, for whatever reason, is classed as an alternative investment option. The gold market operates completely differently to the second-hand celebrity tissue market, so there's no one-size-fits-all rule here.

4. Time

Time really is money when it comes to investments. Very broadly speaking, you shouldn't be investing money you might need in the next five years, or longer. That's because the value of anything you invest in can go up or down over weeks and months. So the longer you invest in a diverse set of assets, the better chance your money has of growing.

You can invest a lump sum every now and then or take the little and often approach, which means you're getting into a routine and factoring it into your budget. Being consistent with investing is important – sometimes even more so than the sums you invest. That's because you can benefit from the averaging effect: when you regularly invest the same amount of money over time, you don't need to obsess about 'timing' the market or worry about share price or market fluctuations. By starting now (even if you're starting small), you're giving your money extra time to ride out the usual ups and downs in the market – and benefit from potential dividends, yields and compounding!

The S&P 500

The S&P 500 is a stock market index that tracks the performance of 500 of the largest companies in the US. And if you look at how it's done over the last 40 years, you'll see that even though there are dips here and there, it's been on the rise. There have been shock moments, like the financial crisis in 2008, which caused global market crashes. Even though the market eventually 'recovered' and continued growing, you would have seen a sharp drop in the value of your investments if you'd put your money in companies or funds that were exposed to the damage. And if you took your money out for whatever reason at that time – for example, if you were on the brink of retirement and had expected it to be part of your income – you would have suffered losses. Those fluctuations are impossible to predict, because they're influenced by things like politics, economics and corporate strategy. Not even the most seasoned investors can see into the future, which is why 'timing' the market rarely works in practice.

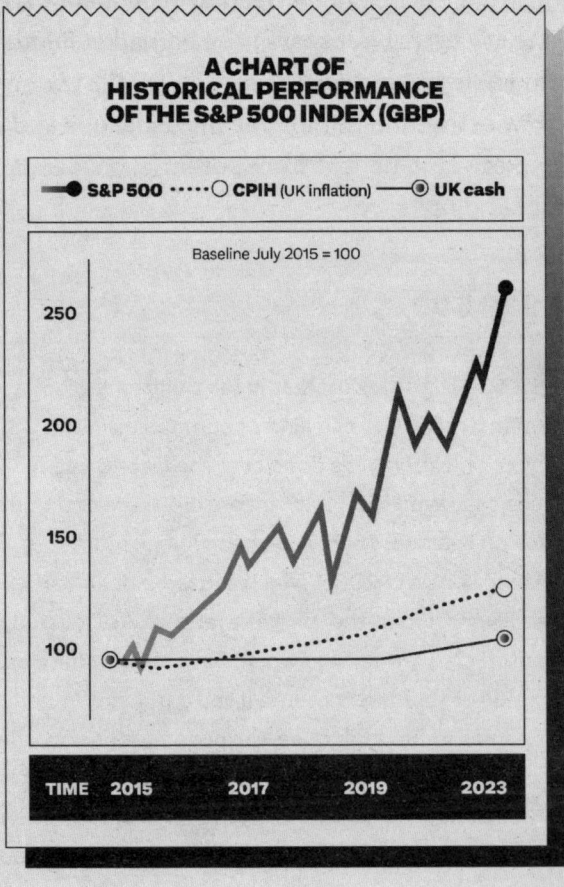

A CHART OF HISTORICAL PERFORMANCE OF THE S&P 500 INDEX (GBP)

● **S&P 500**   ○ **CPIH** (UK inflation)   ◉ **UK cash**

Baseline July 2015 = 100

250

200

150

100

TIME   2015   2017   2019   2023

UK inflation, cash rates and stock indexes from 2015 to 2024. Sourced from BOE (Cash Rate, CFMB2HW),[11] ONS (CPIH, cpih01),[12] Yahoo! Finance (S&P).[13]

5. Feelings

Investing is heavily influenced by how people feel. Because, as much as we wish we could, we can't know exactly how an investment will do – there's always a degree of the unknown attached. And depending on how that makes you feel, you might be more or less willing to embrace risk when it comes to investments. The golden rule is not to make investment decisions based on emotional reactions when you're faced with a volatile, ever-changing market. It's easier said than done, but staying cool, calm and collected will help you avoid withdrawing your investments at a bad time in the market.

Numbers and feelings

The stock market is a good example of how people, numbers and uncertainty mix together. Studies have shown that investors might be more optimistic when the weather improves![14] A stock exchange might look like it's all numbers and graphs, but it's really just a massive crowd of people (and algorithms created by people) reacting to stuff. They can get skittish when things look uncertain, or they think there's a risk they'll lose lots of money (also known as 'being spooked'). If the market starts to think a stock is going to lose value, people rush to sell their holdings in that stock before it becomes worth less – or worthless. Ironically, this makes it worth *even less*, because everyone's rushing to sell it. Remember, it's just as important to do your research before selling an investment as it is before buying one.

How you can actually start

Like we said, you can invest in pretty much anything, from fine wine to collectible action figures. But unless you're a trained sommelier or have an intimate knowledge of the Marvel universe, you'll likely find your start through some ready-made options that either a person or computer algorithm creates for you.

Browsing your options

As a newbie, you're most likely to get your start through a bank or an investment platform. They connect you to some of the options out there, but not before you open an investment account and go through ID checks and answer some questions on your risk appetite. Your bank might have a few packaged, ready-made investments to choose from, which can help narrow down the options for you. Investment platforms are like virtual supermarkets, where you can choose from literally thousands of investment options. We've already touched on a few of the ones they might have in there – like stocks and shares – and we'll explain how some of those get bundled together now.

Choosing your investment wrapper

We introduced you to tax wrappers in the 'Strategies for saving' chapter, and they exist in the world of investments too! They're the gift that keeps on giving, protecting your account from income or capital gains tax (a tax on profits you make when you sell an asset that's increased in value). A stocks and shares ISA is similar to a cash ISA, and lets you invest tax-free, which is why it's often people's first port of call. Remember, you're currently allowed to save or invest a total of £20,000 tax-free per tax year across both a cash ISA and a stocks and shares ISA. You can decide how you want to split the £20,000 between them. If you use up your ISA allowance in a tax year, there are other wrappers you can use for your investments. You can keep investing using a general investment account (GIA) – just keep in mind those investments won't be tax-free. A pension is also a tax wrapper, which we'll get into in the 'Life after work' chapter. And when we say you can start investing early, we mean really early! Stocks and shares junior ISAs let parents invest on behalf of their kids. The yearly tax-free allowance for these is currently £9,000, and even a modest £10 per month throughout a childhood means compounding can work its magic for *even* longer.

Investing in funds

There are investment platforms out there that'll let you invest in individual shares, bonds and other investments yourself. But if you want someone to make the decisions for you, you might want to consider a fund. A fund is a way of pooling your money with others to invest in a diverse range of assets. Funds are managed by a professional fund manager or an algorithm created by a professional, and they decide on a mix of assets to invest in for you. There are funds that are themed around countries or certain industries, and others that mix together lots of different assets. Some funds even invest in other funds. There could also be funds that *avoid* certain industries, like fossil fuels or tobacco. You might have heard of environmental, social and governance (ESG) funds that invest in ethical companies and projects.

There are also exchange-traded funds (known as ETFs), which are another type of fund where you buy and sell the units of the ETF (basically the same as shares) on a stock exchange, just like you would buy and sell shares in a company. ETFs are designed to reflect particular investment principles. Some try to track the performance of a specific stock market index (like the S&P 500 we talked about earlier), some hold a group of different investments, like shares, bonds and more. And an ETF that tracks an index aims to rise and fall in value in the same way as the investments in that index. Like other types of funds, ETFs can be popular because they make it easy to invest in a diverse range of things and can sometimes charge lower fees than other types of funds.

The whole point of funds is to package up diverse investment options for you, and each fund will have a clear risk rating attached to it. Keep in mind the key concepts that underpin all investing when you're picking a fund, or any investment option: risk, timing, volatility, diversifying your portfolio, and feelings. There's literally thousands of funds for you to choose from – more than 4,700 to be exact;[15] roughly the number of times we've written the word 'fund' in this paragraph.

Active and passive funds

Professional investment strategists manage active funds, and their entire job is choosing what to invest in for you. Some of the most successful fund managers have an almost celebrity status in the financial world (so don't be surprised if you find yourself chasing one down for an autograph after getting into investing). If you invest in an active fund, you're paying higher fund management fees for them and their teams to analyse a huge amount of information and buy and sell stocks, sometimes even daily. Their aim is to make you more money and 'outperform' the market.

The other sort is a 'passive' fund. This is where fund managers check your investments regularly and track the performance of whole markets, rather than individual stocks. They generally have lower fees attached to them than active funds do. A common type is a tracker fund that lets you invest in all the companies that make up an index all at once, like the US S&P 500. Some companies in an index will rise in value and some won't, and a tracker fund covers all of them, so your money is pegged to the overall performance of a market.

There's plenty of debate around which type of fund is a 'better' investment. Ultimately, they're both different by design – active funds try to outperform the market, while passive funds try to keep up with it. According to studies, there's no right or wrong answer.[16] If you're investing in any kind of fund, you'll have to pay an annual fund management charge and transaction costs whenever you or your fund manager buys or sells assets. The fees attached to passive funds are generally much lower, which is a useful thing to keep in mind.

Case study

'I didn't think investing was for me, but now I get it.'

Natalie, 38, is an event planner from London. Her best friend Michael works in banking, and there's been a lot of investment talk in their WhatsApp chat lately. Investing is something Natalie really wants to engage with but doesn't know heaps about. She asks Michael how to get going, and he suggests that she start small, only risk what she's willing to lose, and continue to pay into her savings account too.

Feeling excited that she has a clear plan, Natalie opens

her banking app and transfers £100 into a savings pot with a 3.8% interest rate, and £100 into a managed investment pot, picking an 'adventurous' fund from a range offered by a well-regarded provider. Although she's a little cautious, she feels comfortable now she understands the risks – she's prepared for the fact the invested £100 may go down in value, and doesn't need that money any time soon.

At the end of the first month, Natalie has £100.32 in savings, and £105.60 (5.6% growth in one month) in her investment pot. In the second month, the savings are up to £100.64, while the investment pot pulls back to £102 (a 3.4% decline in growth from month to month). She decides to leave the pots alone for a bit to do their thing. Five months later, she returns to £102.23 in her savings and £109.85 in the investment pot. Despite the ups and downs, the investment is up 2.5%.

Natalie started to see the difference in growth rate between savings and investments: one was steady but relatively modest, while the other was inconsistent but higher overall. Once Natalie felt more confident, the next step was to develop a system to contribute to her investments regularly. Her plan was to continue prioritising her savings and then top up her investments with anything left over from her categorised pots at the end of each month (she's a big fan of the envelope budgeting method!). For example, if she underspends on eating out, she'll pop the excess money into her investments. Sometimes it's nothing, sometimes it's £50, sometimes it's even as high as £120!

Two years later, Natalie has £2,126 in her investment pot at a compounding growth rate of 11.94%. She's now created space in her monthly budget to set up a direct debit for £50 a month as a regular contribution.

Investing in individual shares

You might be wondering how you can invest in individual companies – you know, the ones who are so successful they can afford ads at half-time when the Euros are on. If you invest in individual company shares, you'll be doing what's called share dealing. You can do it with as little as £50–100 nowadays, by buying 'fractional shares'. That's when you own part of a share in a publicly traded company. By choosing to do share dealing, you're putting your faith in individual companies doing well over time. That's not guaranteed for all sorts of reasons, which is why it's riskier to invest in just one company than it is to invest in different companies, sectors and types of assets.

Cryptocurrency

You've probably already heard of cryptocurrency, or crypto – the new kid on the block. Named after the Greek prefix for 'hidden or secret', it's a currency bound up in computer code that isn't owned by any country or bank. Its creators hoped that one day, crypto would replace pounds, dollars and yen. But there was a snag – unless you went to a super techy café most likely located in Silicon Valley, you couldn't actually use it to buy stuff. And even if you did find a café whose clientele dreamed in zeros and ones, you'd need a 'crypto wallet'.

What came next was a subtle but very important shift. Instead of currency you can use, crypto became a thing you could invest in. Bitcoin, the first and now most famous cryptocurrency, skyrocketed in value and its success spawned thousands of new cryptocurrencies, each with their own purpose and value.

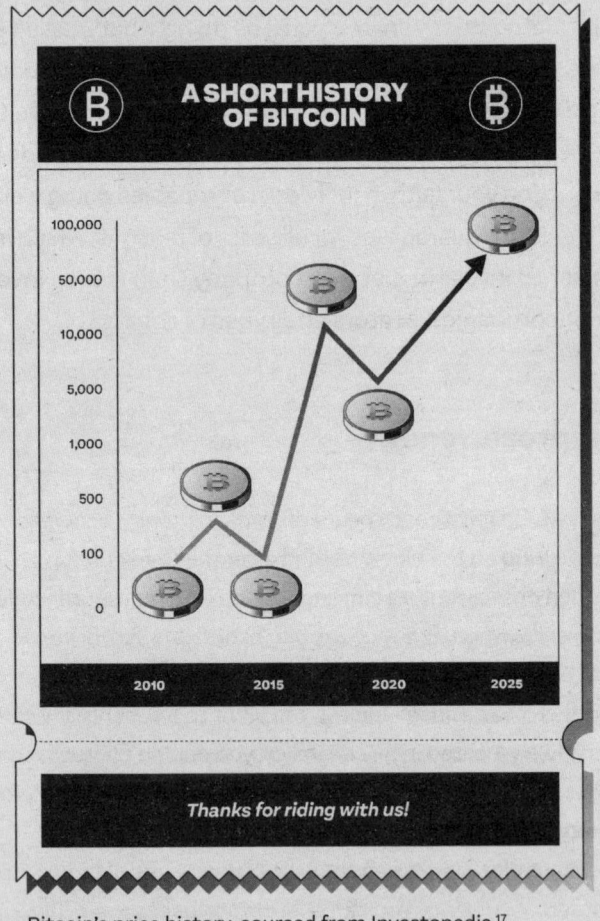

Bitcoin's price history, sourced from Investopedia.[17]

Our customers tell us that crypto is one of the main types of investments they're curious about, and it's not surprising. Stories of people losing and gaining lots of money trading crypto have an almost thrilling quality. Because of all that mystique, you might have found you're unclear on what it *actually* is.

Cryptocurrencies aren't official currencies as far as the British government is concerned, so regulators classify them instead under 'crypto assets'. Crypto is legal to buy, own and sell, and if you buy crypto and sell it at a profit, you'd usually need to pay capital gains tax. But be aware that crypto remains largely unregulated and high risk. Crypto can be a pretty volatile investment option for lots of reasons – it hasn't been around long, and is super reactive to unusual things like social posts from famous people. Some add it to their investments portfolio as a bit of a risky wildcard. Experts' wisdom generally says no more than 5% of the cash you have set aside towards investing goes towards high-risk assets,[18] and you need to be emotionally and financially prepared to lose it all.

You can invest in Bitcoin and other cryptocurrencies through specialised platforms that offer them. There are more than 25,000 cryptocurrencies, so make sure you know which one you're investing in. Some traditional fund managers are also starting to hold established cryptocurrencies like Bitcoin and shares of crypto exchanges in their funds. Those will be higher risk than the funds we talked about earlier, but lower risk than investing directly in a single crypto asset, as you'll be benefiting from a diversified fund. Just remember, crypto is relatively new and unknown, so it's hard to say where it will be in 10 months, let alone 10 years. Investing your future fund in an unpredictable asset like crypto is extremely risky, because you could lose it all.

How much should I invest? (And how much does it cost?)

Our research shows that by far the biggest barrier to investing is feeling like you don't have enough cash. But there are plenty of online platforms where you can start with as little as a pound! Investing lives in that section of your budget that's devoted to looking after your future self. And doing it in smaller amounts regularly is better than not investing at all, which is why it helps to think of it as just another line in your monthly outgoings. When it comes to exactly how much you should invest, keep in mind:

- Where you can make some trade-offs to create more room in your budget for investing. If investing £50 a month means you sacrifice one nice dinner or 166 Freddos a month, it's probably worth doing.
- How comfortable you feel about losing that money (your risk appetite).
- How much money you're comfortable not having access to for the next five years.

It's a good idea to pay off any high-interest debt and create a savings safety net before you become a regular investor, and it's a bad idea to use a credit card to invest. Setting up a regular contribution to an investment pot means you won't even have to think about it.

Investing comes with fees attached

The cost of investing becomes important as your investment pot grows, so it's good to keep an eye on the fees that eat into your returns. If you choose to invest through an investment platform, you'll typically pay a platform fee to access them and, on top of that, a fund management fee for each fund you have. These are the main fees you might come across:

- Platform fees can be a monthly or yearly subscription to maintain your account. This can be a fixed amount, or it can be a percentage of the portfolio. The key is to choose a platform with competitive costs and a fee structure you understand.
- If you invest in funds, there's usually also an annual fund management charge, most likely a percentage of your invested balance. Actively managed funds charge higher fees – typically 0.75% to 1.5% (and some even higher) of your invested balance. Passive funds charge lower fees; some tracker funds can be as low as 0.01% to 0.85%. For example: if you've got £1,000 in a fund that charges 0.75%, they'll charge you £7.50 per year in fees. That may not seem much right now, but when the pot grows

more and more, so do the fees. And you still pay those fees no matter what, even if the fund doesn't perform well enough to give you any returns.

The Capital Grille
280310 Treasury Terrace,
Goldenfields, GF9 2XP, United Kingdom

TAKEAWAYS

ITEM	QTY
Invest for the long term	1
Start as soon as you're ready	1
Diversify	1
Prioritise your peace of mind	1
TOTAL	**4**

TAKEAWAYS

Invest for the long term: savings will get you far, but they won't protect you from inflation. Think of your investment timeline in years, not months. The longer you invest, the better chance you have of your investments growing.

Start as soon as you're ready: investments need time, so start as soon as you're in a position to, and be consistent! Use the 50–30–20 rule from the 'Balancing your budget' chapter to make room in your budget for investments if you can, even if it's not much.

Diversify: there are literally countless types of investments you can make. Do your research into the opportunities and only invest in what you understand. Although it can be overwhelming at first, it's how you can spread and manage risk.

Prioritise your peace of mind: investing 'well' isn't just about growing financial assets, it's about your peace of mind. Investments can be emotionally challenging, which is why it's really important to understand your own tolerance for risk. Investing in less risky options that won't grow as fast is better than not investing at all. You don't need to beat the market, you just need to know how to benefit from it.

When I say I'm in a long-term relationship, I mean my 12-month contract (no break clause)

Chapter 9
Making the most of home and renting

When *Location, Location, Location* first aired in 2000, even its presenters didn't expect it to make it past the pilot episode. Forty seasons in, it's safe to say the show isn't going anywhere. There's nothing Brits love more than a creaky fixer-upper on *Homes Under the Hammer*, except for maybe an architectural masterpiece on *Grand Designs* that goes outrageously over budget.

More and more people are turning to social media to get their fix, too. Creators and estate agents have been quick to hop on the trend, using platforms like TikTok to show off, and even sell, homes. As of 2024, posts with the #ukhousetour tag had nearly 16 million views[1] and posts with the hashtag #property had over 8.5 *billion*.[2]

Are we just nosy, or massive fans of interior design? Probably both! There's nothing better than poking around a friend's flat, except for maybe curating Pinterest boards with titles like 'Mid-century modern chic' or 'Beach cottage core'. But despite our national obsession, the realities of renting and buying can be far from Pinterest-perfect. For 76% of people, buying a house is the dream.[3] And while it's not an impossible one, it's more difficult than ever.[4]

How we live is changing. Back in 2000, the average deposit for a first-time buyer was around £13,000, and the average house price was £85,000. Fast-forward to 2024 and the average deposit has skyrocketed to £53,000, with average house prices at £290,000 (and even more in London).[5] Because of all that, 18% of 24- to 34-year-olds still live with their parents,[6] a third of people are likely to rent well into retirement,[7] and the average age of a first-time buyer is now 37 – up five years since 2020.[8] Renting has gone from a stopgap in your early 20s to a common long-term arrangement, while buying takes more preparation and willpower than ever. If that's overwhelming to think about, don't worry! We'll go into how to plan and budget for your deposit, then cover the details (and drama) of the house-buying process in the next chapter. For now, we'll take a look at deciding what you want from your home, then dive into the world of renting.

Expectation versus reality

What do you want from a home now, and where do you see yourself in the future? We don't mean the exact shade of off-white you picture for your walls, though that's obviously a crucial decision too. Where you choose to live will depend on your budget, but it also tends to reflect what's important to you. Are you into walks and wide open vistas, or hot new wine bars in the heart of the city? Do you want to be close to family, or as far away as humanly possible? Is home where you occasionally bathe, or where you spend every waking second? There are a thousand tiny personal preferences you might have when it comes to where you live, and you'll want to get as close to your ideal set-up as possible. What you have access to will depend on your income and budget, plus bigger stuff that's out of your hands, like the housing market. But that only makes it more important to focus on what you *can* control.

Grab a paper and pen, or the notes app on your phone, and take some time to reflect on where you're at, what you'd like to change (if anything), and what you can do to make it possible.

Reflections

My current priorities

Take a moment to think about what you want from a home right now. Budget, size, location etc. *For example: 'I'm renting a flat with two friends. I pay £950 a month in rent and £200 in bills, which is about 40% of my salary. My priorities right now include location near the office, keeping living costs down, and saving up for a deposit with my girlfriend.'*

My plans for the future

Think about how your priorities might change in the next few months or years, and what that might mean for you. *For example: 'I'd like to rent a place with my girlfriend in the next couple of years, preferably on a good cycle route, to test out living together before we buy. Willing to trade off location for a little more space.'*

My financial realities

How will you work towards your plans, financially speaking? *For example: 'To live in the area we like, we'll need to save £20,000 each for a deposit. I've already got about £7,000 put away, and Mum and Dad will put in £3,000. So I've got to save about £400 a month if I want to move in two years' time.'*

My must-haves

Rank what's most important to you in a home. This could change over time, so it's worth asking yourself this question regularly. *For example: 'I want to have a short commute and be near fun restaurants/bars in the centre of town.'*

My trade-offs

There are certain things you might have to do without to make the must-haves happen. Think about what those are, and what they might be in the future. *For example: 'Right now, I'm prioritising a city centre location over outdoor space. I don't care that much about it right now, but that'll matter a lot to me in a permanent home.'*

Remember those financial eras we talked about in the introduction? Your housing goals are likely to change as you do. And because it's such a huge milestone (often with a hefty price tag attached) it's really important to think about the long term and how your priorities might shift. You shouldn't have to live miserably now to make the dream happen later, though. As with most things in life, it's all about finding balance and feeling clear on what you want.

Renting

Avocado toast-munching millennials are known as 'gen-eration rent', but in reality a lack of affordable housing has pushed more age groups into long-term renting than ever before. In a way, this shift brings Brits in line with the rest of Europe, where renting is much more common than buying. In places like Germany and the Netherlands, long-term ten-ancies are standard and renting isn't seen as a temporary or second-rate option. But that's because in those places, the system offers a much higher level of protection for tenants, so people can happily rent for life. That's just not the case here – both because the UK rental market doesn't offer that stability, and because buying is still a huge milestone for Brits. Home is where the mortgage is, and where you're finally allowed to put a nail in the wall.

Whatever our cultural perceptions of renting, it's becoming more and more common, and we're doing it for longer than ever before. So it's worth finding stability and comfort in renting, if that's what you want or need to do right now.

Let's start with an honest look at the pros and cons.

The cons

- **Your landlord calls the shots:** tenants do have some protections in the UK, but landlords still make the big decisions. They can raise your rent, sell the property, or decide not to renew your lease, so you're forced to move when you don't want to. That can be stressful and disruptive, impacting things like your kids' education, your job, your commute and your social life.

- **You're not building equity:** 'equity' is basically the part of the property you actually own – it's the difference between its value and what you still owe on the mortgage. A 25-year loan might feel like a lifelong commitment, but each payment inches you closer towards owning the place outright. Renting, on the other hand, is a big outgoing that offers no financial return.

- **It gets more expensive over time:** in the 12 months leading up to July 2024, average rents increased by 8.6% in England, 7.9% in Wales and 8.2% in Scotland.[9] The tricky thing is, this increase isn't always something you can plan for. With a mortgage, you have the option to fix your monthly repayments for a number of years, but rent can generally increase every six to 12 months.

- **Limited creative control:** renting means that big changes, like replacing an old bathroom, are usually off the table. And even small touches, like painting the front door hot coral, might need your landlord's blessing. Some people are happy to leave maintenance to their landlord, others not so much.

The pros

- **It's a building block:** renting is where many people start and it teaches you life skills that'll serve you in the future, like how to budget for your monthly rent, pay bills on time, and fit a bottom sheet on your own. It's also an affordable way to get a taste of that sweet, sweet freedom and independence when you're ready to fly the family nest.

- **Flexibility:** you can hop to a new neighbourhood as soon as your lease is up. Perfect if a job opportunity takes you to a different city, or you just want the option to explore. It's also a great way to test the waters of living with friends or a partner. After all, you don't want to be tied down with someone who leaves wet towels on the floor.

- **Lower upfront costs:** there aren't any mandatory legal fees or hefty deposits in the tens of thousands – you usually need one month's rent upfront, which you should get back if you leave the property in a good state.

- **Your landlord covers the fixes:** as a tenant, you're spared the home repairs that can drain your safety net in an instant. Major plumbing disaster? Boiler on the blink? Those are, legally speaking, your landlord's problem.

Getting the most out of renting

Renting can be a necessary step, or even a valid destination. And there are some practical things you can do to maximise the pros and minimise the cons. Here are three golden rules that'll help give you the stability and protection you need.

Golden rule 1: know your rights

The first golden rule? Knowing the rules. And they change often. Citizens Advice and the housing and homeless charity Shelter always have the most up-to-date information on your rights as a tenant. But generally speaking these are some things you might want to watch out for:

- Make sure your landlord or letting agent puts your deposit in a protection scheme that's recognised by the government. Currently that's MyDeposits, the Deposit Protection Service, the Tenancy Deposit Scheme, Letting Protection Service Scotland, SafeDeposits Scotland and MyDeposits Scotland.
- Read your contract carefully and look out for things that seem odd, like rules that feel unfair or charges that seem excessively high. It's not as fun as picking the perfect new bedsheets, but you'll be glad you did it.
- If something's broken, a landlord has to fix it in a reasonable timeframe, so make sure you're firm but fair if things are moving slowly. And remember to take pictures of anything that looks broken on the day you move in, then email them to your landlord. You're creating a paper trail you can pull up if they claim you damaged something.

Rogue landlords exist and they rely on a lack of knowledge and experience to overcharge for repairs or withhold deposits. That's why keeping up to date with the latest rules matters.

And don't forget to check if you're entitled to Universal Credit, which has replaced Housing Benefit. This is a monthly payment (or twice a month for some people in Scotland) from the government that helps you with living costs like your rent. You may be entitled to it if you're on a low income or out of work. And if you live on your own, you might also qualify for a single person's discount on your council tax, which will save you 25% on your bill (this discount applies whether you rent or own your home). Visit the government website for the latest on both of these things, as the rules sometimes change.

Golden rule 2: vet your flatmates

Living with friends isn't always as idyllic as the friends from *Friends* made it look. Choose potential flatmates wisely and make sure you're on the same page about leaving dishes in the sink overnight. Have a conversation upfront to agree on how you want to split chores, bills and fridge space. Who knows, you might be the first people in history to success- fully stick to a cleaning rota! More seriously, if you're on a joint tenancy together (that's a contract with all your signed names on it), you're all responsible, and will all face the consequences if one of you doesn't pay, or somebody breaks something. For example, you could end up having to cover someone else's share of the rent if they don't pay up. You might get on with someone really well at the pub, but living with them is another thing entirely, so it's important to trust that the people you live with are safe, sound and financially stable.

Golden rule 3: don't let a good thing go

If you've hit the renting jackpot (great place, price, location, landlord and flatmates), try to introduce stability to your situation. Keep a solid relationship with your landlord or letting agent – if they're reasonable, they'll value a reliable tenant. Ask for a longer contract period to keep rent locked in at your current price, and report problems quickly. It'll help build trust between you and your landlord or agent, which can only be a good thing.

Case study

'Can I face moving back into my childhood bedroom?'

Meet Maja, an architect who's been living and renting in London for over a decade.

Through her twenties, Maja lived in eight different house shares around the city. Some parts have been great. She made new friends, and sampled pastries and coffees in all four corners of London. She's a big fan of the Beatles and even got the chance to live on Abbey Road. Other parts were hellishly stressful. There was the pianist housemate she found on SpareRoom who felt most inspired to practise their craft after midnight. And that time she had to move herself and her extensive collection of hardbacks from Bermondsey to Stratford on the hottest day of the year.

Eventually, Maja grew tired of having to share a home with strangers from the internet. When she got a promotion at work, she decided to increase her housing budget so she could experience the joys of living by herself. While she no longer had to chip in to a communal shop that funded her ex-flatmate's expensive taste in 12-ply toilet roll, she found managing bills alone stressful, and much pricier. But once she got to grips with the bill admin and made use of her single person's Council Tax discount, Maja fell in love with having her own space.

It motivated her to start thinking seriously about saving up for a deposit on her own flat – one where she could finally paint the walls a statement colour. But she knew it'd only be possible if she moved back in with her parents. Luckily they only lived an hour outside London, but it'd mean losing her new-found independence.

Maja already had £10,000 saved in an ISA, but needed an extra £20,000 to reach her deposit goal of £30,000. So she broke down how long it would take to reach her target if she moved back home. You can see her calculations on page 181.

She knew she was fortunate to have the option. But in the end, she couldn't face moving back into her childhood bedroom and staring at her old *Twilight* posters while dialling into work calls. Even though it would take her an extra three years to save enough, she decided it was worth it to keep her independence. In the meantime, there was another promotion at work she decided to go for, which would help her get there quicker.

MAJA'S PROPOSAL

RENTING

Salary: .... **£45,000 per year**

Monthly take-home pay: **£2,939**

Rent: .... **£1,560 per month**

Living costs: .... **£979 per month**

Amount she could save
for her deposit: .... **£400 per month**

Time to deposit: .... **just over four years**

MOVING BACK HOME

Salary: .... **£45,000 per year**

Monthly take-home pay: **£2,939**

Contributing to bills and food
shops at home: .... **£350 per month**

Living costs: .... **£979 per month**

Amount she could save
for her deposit: .... **£1,610 per month**

Time to deposit: .... **just over a year**

Lease & Latte
2109 Tenant Terrace,
Lettingsbury, LN4 8RE, United Kingdom

TAKEAWAYS

ITEM	QTY
Work out what you want most from your home	1
Know your rights	1
Find stability and comfort in renting	1
TOTAL	**3**

HAVE A NICE DAY

TAKEAWAYS

Work out what you want most from your home: it's unlikely you'll be able to get everything on your wish list, so think about what you're prepared to compromise on to get what you want. This is especially true if you're working towards the goal of buying a house, which we'll talk more about in the next chapter.

Know your rights: make sure that your landlord or estate agent puts your deposit in a protection scheme and read your contract carefully.

Find stability and comfort in renting: renting might feel temporary because of cultural perceptions, but it's important that where you live feels like a real home. If you've found a great place at an affordable price that meets your needs, try to introduce stability to your situation by asking for a longer contract and building a good relationship with your agent or landlord.

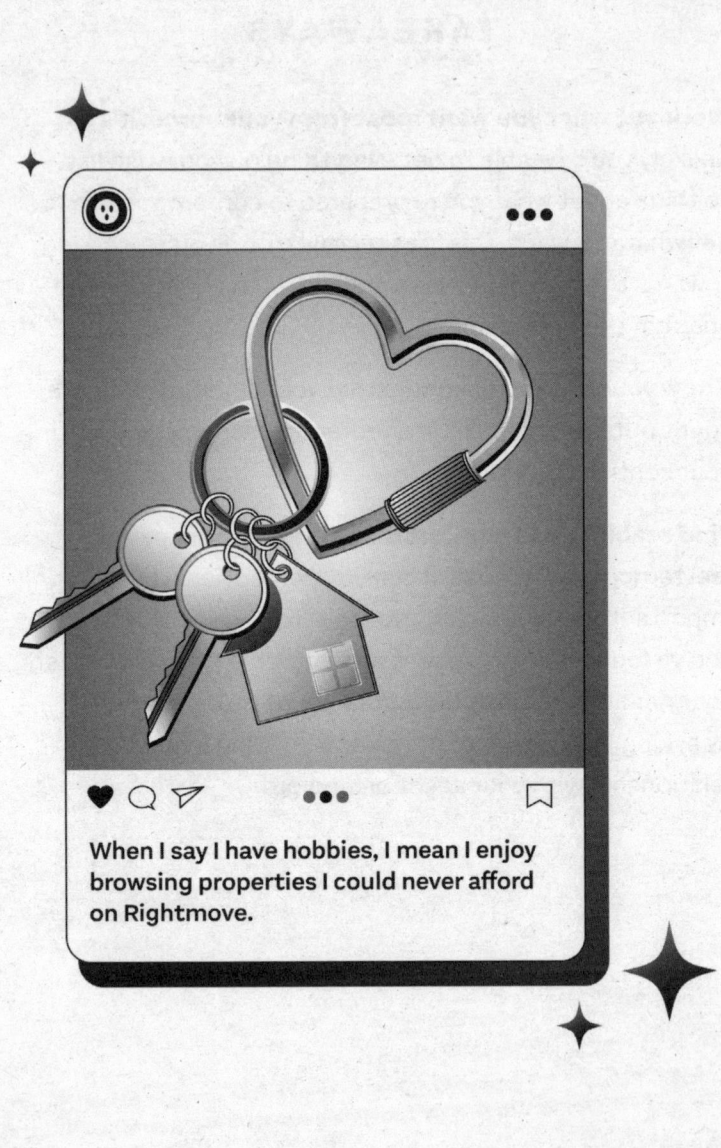

When I say I have hobbies, I mean I enjoy browsing properties I could never afford on Rightmove.

Chapter 10
Buying a home

Your home is probably the most expensive thing you'll ever buy, and is likely to be the biggest loan you'll ever take out. The huge challenge of saving up your deposit and paying Stamp Duty, and all the steps that follow – from viewings and offers to legal paperwork – can feel pretty confusing and chaotic, especially if you're a first-time buyer.

But the pay-off? It *almost* makes the whole thing worth it. Because once you climb Savings Mountain and make it through the Paperwork Maze, you end up with a place where you can paint the walls whatever colour you want – and where the only annoying landlord you have to deal with is yourself on a hangover. But before you start shopping for a brand new sofa, it pays to know what to expect from the process. Life isn't always as neat and methodical as a numbered list – you might skip ahead on some steps or have to repeat others – but generally, it goes like this . . .

Step 1: sort out your spending

It's never too early to get a handle on your debt and spending because, when the time comes, lenders will take a good look at your credit report and bank statements. They basically do this to make sure the information you've provided about your earnings is correct, and you'll be able to keep up with the monthly mortgage repayments. This doesn't mean they're judging your daily triple shot venti iced caramel macchiato with oat milk, but try to live within your means and avoid any big splurges.

Step 2: work out your affordability

Another early step is working out your 'affordability' – what you can afford to borrow based on your deposit, income and outgoings.

Lenders will typically have a maximum amount they're willing to lend to you, which is normally around four times your income, but can occasionally go up to five or six times if you're a higher earner. Things can be a little more complicated if you're self-employed or rely heavily on bonuses and commission, but you can get a mortgage broker to help you (more on them later) or play around with an online mortgage calculator to see your options.

As well as looking at your current situation, you could try tweaking the numbers to fit future scenarios. For example: *how much more would the bank lend me if I got a 3% pay rise?*

What if I boosted my deposit by an extra £2,000? How would these numbers change if I bought with someone else? At this stage, you might not be looking for a super accurate answer, but it can help you understand how close you are to your home-buying goal, and what adjustments you could make to get there.

Step 3: save for your deposit, Stamp Duty and other costs

Saving enough to cover the upfront costs of buying a home is probably the biggest hurdle most people face. It requires serious discipline, a clear plan and a fair bit of sacrifice. Before we go any further, let's take a look at how much you're likely to need.

As a general rule of thumb, first-time buyers need a deposit of roughly 5% of the property's value. If you're going for a buy-to-let, it's usually between 25% and 40%. If you already own a home and you've decided to sell up and move, the process is a bit different. Buying your next home usually means getting a new mortgage and going through the process again, especially if you're moving to a more expensive place and need to borrow more money. However, if your current mortgage allows it, you might be able to transfer or 'port' it over to your new property. (You'll still need to reapply for it, though.) And don't forget, if your current home has equity, this can go towards the deposit on your new place.

If you're aiming for a 5% deposit, just bear in mind that because it's the minimum amount, you'll have fewer lenders to choose from and will likely be hit with their most expensive interest rates. If you're able to *increase* your deposit to above 5% of the property's value, then you'll get access to better rates because you'll be borrowing less – making lending to you less of a risk. But of course, for a lot of people that just isn't possible, which is why many aim for the 5% target.

When you're working out how much you need, it's important to factor in costs beyond your deposit, so they don't catch you out. Stamp Duty is a big one you may have to factor in. But what actually is it? When it comes to property, 'Stamp Duty' normally refers to one of three taxes: Stamp Duty Land Tax in England and Northern Ireland, Land and Buildings Transaction Tax in Scotland, and Land Transaction Tax in Wales. It's based on the purchase price of the property – the higher the value, the higher the amount you'll need to pay. You'll also have to pay extra if you're buying an additional property, like a second home or a buy-to-let. So when you're saving, make sure you factor it in. Like other sorts of tax, you won't have to pay below a certain threshold, which varies depending on where you are in the UK. You might also be exempt if you're a first-time buyer. These rules can change, so be sure to check out the latest information on the government website.

There are other add-on costs we'll touch on later, so it's always a good idea to build in a generous buffer on the amount you're planning to save.

The lowdown on LTV

You might come across a term called loan to value (LTV), which mortgage lenders use to set their interest rates based on how much you'd be borrowing as a percentage of your home's value. If your LTV is higher, your interest is likely to be higher too.

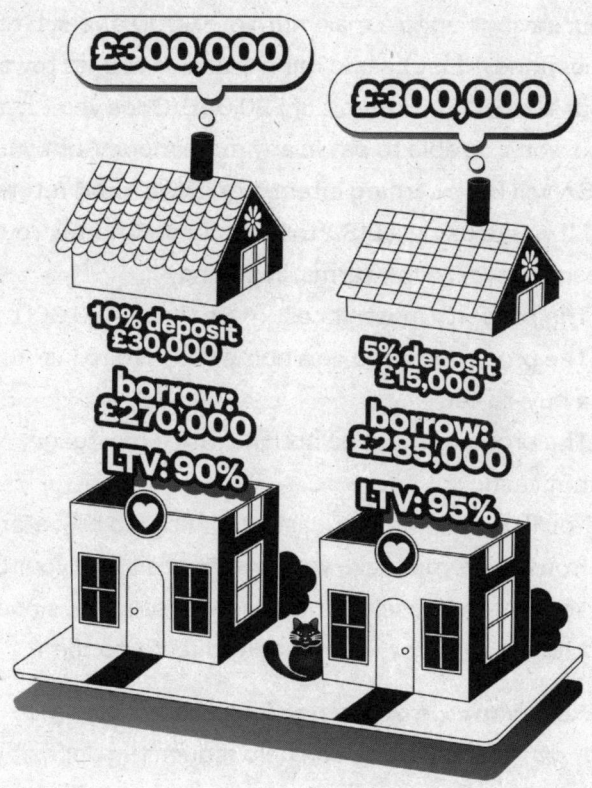

Whether you're almost at your deposit target, or you're starting from scratch, there are ways to make your money go further and help you reach your goal more quickly:

- **Look into a LISA:** a lifetime ISA – or a LISA – is a special kind of ISA designed to help you buy your first home or save money for later life. You can open a LISA if you're aged 18 to 39, and you can put in up to £4,000 each year until you're 50. The government will add a 25% bonus to your savings up to a maximum of £1,000 a year. Literally free money! Just bear in mind that this counts towards your annual ISA tax limit of £20,000. Once you turn 50, you won't be able to pay in any more money, but your LISA will keep earning interest or investment returns.

    If you're using a LISA to buy your first home, you'll need to follow a few terms, including:
    - The property mustn't cost more than £450,000.
    - The property has to be a home you plan to live in, not a buy-to-let.
    - The property must be bought with a mortgage, not cash.
    - You'll need to wait at least 12 months to buy, starting from when you make your first deposit into your LISA.
    - You'll have to use a conveyancer or solicitor, since the LISA provider pays the money directly to them.

- **Take advantage of government schemes:** some government schemes can help reduce the deposit you need. With 'shared ownership', for example, you only buy a share of the property – usually between 25% and 75% – and rent the rest from a housing association. This means you only need a mortgage on the percentage you own. The deposit is typically around 5% of the value of your share. So, if the property costs £200,000 and you buy a 50% share, your share would be worth £100,000. And you'd need £5,000 for a 5% deposit. Over time, you can choose to increase the percentage you own and, in turn, reduce the rent you pay. This can be a great option if you're buying alone, or earn a lower income and are struggling to save up. But there are some possible downsides to consider. For example, selling up can be trickier (housing associations can set some restrictions), and you'll still need to pay rent on the part you don't own, which can add up over time. So do some research to figure out if it's the right option for you.

- **Make it multi-player:** buying a place on your own is a challenge, from a financial standpoint and emotionally, too. If you're flying solo, you should be proud of yourself. But if you're finding it difficult, there are lots of arrangements you could consider to lighten the load, like buying with a sibling or friends. The lender TSB found that 57% of all their first-time buyers were with more than one applicant.[1] If you pool your resources with others, the obvious benefit is you'll have more money to play with.

If you do take the plunge with someone else, you'll need to decide whether you want to be 'joint tenants' or 'tenants in common'. (Heads up: the rules and terminology are a little different in Scotland.) Joint tenants means the property belongs to all owners equally. In this set-up, you can't remortgage or sell up without everyone's agreement, and you can't give away a share of the property in your will. If you die, the property passes automatically to the other owners. Tenants in common means you each own a specific share of the property's value, and everyone's share can be different. Usually, it's based on how much money you each put into the deposit and mortgage repayments. If you die, you can leave your share to whoever you like in your will.

- **The Bank of Mum & Dad (or older sister, auntie, uncle . . .):** every generation claims to have had it harder than the last, but the truth is it has never been more difficult to get on the property ladder. Rising house prices, low wage growth and skyrocketing mortgage rates have left a lot of people feeling pretty hopeless. Often a helping hand is the only way to get into the market, with one in three first-time buyers relying on support from their families[2] – making the Bank of Mum & Dad one of the UK's biggest lenders.[3]

  This doesn't necessarily mean parents (or other family members) are parting with a hefty chunk of cash, never to be seen again. This support can come in lots of different forms – some people put measures in place to pay their families back over time, while others might go into joint ownership with the person who's helping them. There are also products like 'family assist' mortgages, which let your family use some of their savings as 'security' for your mortgage. In this set-up, their money stays in their bank account but is effectively 'locked off' so they can't use it. They'll be able to access it again depending on the terms of your mortgage – it might be once you pay off a certain amount, or after an agreed length of time. (As long as you keep up to date with your repayments.)

It might feel awkward to ask your family for help, or feel unfair if your parents aren't in a position to. Money is an awkward topic anyway, and adding family into the mix can make it even more uncomfortable. But the truth is, intergenerational wealth plays a huge role in getting on the property ladder right now, whether or not we'd like to admit it. Remember, your friends with that lovely garden flat may well have benefited from a helping hand – not everyone will tell you that they've had support.

Step 4: find a mortgage broker you trust

Buying a home can feel like navigating a maze blindfolded, which is where a mortgage broker comes in. They guide you straight to potential lenders by tracking down the best deal, helping you fill out paperwork, and saving you from hours of online research and complicated legal jargon. So it's no surprise that around 70% of UK buyers used one, with 91% saying it was a good experience.[4]

And it's not just admin. A good mortgage broker will also listen to your worries, answer your questions and steady your nerves. Whether you're salaried or self-employed, they can pinpoint which lenders are most likely to give you the green light. For example, they'll know which ones will treat your overtime or bonuses more generously. Without their expertise, you might waste time applying to lenders who will ghost you faster than a bad date.

The best part? Most mortgage brokers are paid by lenders, so unless they tell you otherwise there's no direct cost to you. Just make sure to double-check with them first. And don't be surprised if you end up ringing them more than your parents when the admin heats up.

What kind of mortgage do I need?

Before we go any further, let's take a moment to run through mortgages and the different features associated with them.

Repayment mortgages

Sometimes known as 'capital and interest' mortgages, this is where you pay back both the loan amount (the 'capital') and the interest over a set period (known as the 'term'). Your monthly repayments include both the capital

What kind

# of mortgage

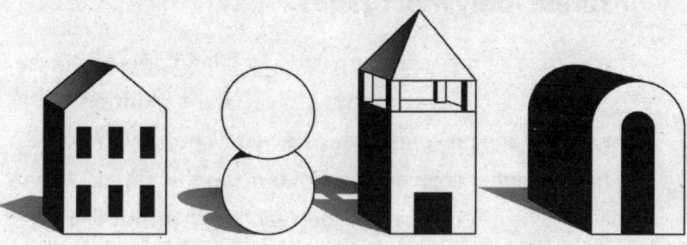

do I need?

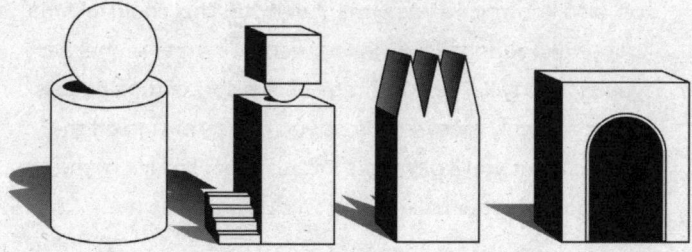

and interest, and by the end of the term you'll have paid back both and own your property outright.

Early on, you might feel like you're barely making any progress. That's because most of your initial monthly repayments go towards paying the interest, rather than the loan itself. But as the years go on, while your monthly repayments will stay the same, more of it will go towards paying off the actual loan. *Overpaying* is a way to get there even faster (more on that later). And you'll also have to make a choice about which sort of interest rate you'll pay.

Interest-only mortgages

These are a lot less common (although landlords often use them for buy-to-let properties). If you want an interest-only mortgage on your home, then you'll normally need to have a higher than average income. In this set-up, you only pay the interest on the loan each month, *not* the actual loan amount. So at the end of the mortgage term, you'll still need to pay back the full amount you borrowed. Lenders usually need to see that you have a plan to pay this off, also known as a 'repayment vehicle'. This could include things like your pension, investments or other properties you plan to sell. The advantage of this sort of mortgage is lower monthly repayments, as you're only paying off the interest, but you'll pay more interest over the life of the mortgage as your balance isn't reducing over time.

Other types of mortgages

- **Buy-to-let mortgages:** if you're planning to rent a property out rather than live in it yourself, you'll need to apply for a buy-to-let mortgage. You'll need a higher deposit than you would for a mortgage on your own home – typically at least 25% to qualify. Some lenders will base this on a percentage of the predicted rental income.

- **Offset mortgages:** these are designed for people with lots of money in savings who don't want to permanently overpay or reduce their mortgage using those savings, but want to reduce their monthly mortgage repayments in the meantime. When you take out an offset mortgage, you'll be given a special account to keep your savings in. Here's an example of how it works: if you placed £50,000 in your offset savings account, your monthly mortgage repayment would be temporarily calculated as if your mortgage was £50,000 lower – therefore saving you money each month. Although it gives you more flexibility to add and remove money, you won't earn any interest on money held in the savings account. Plus, offset mortgages normally have higher fees and interest rates attached to them.

- **Islamic mortgages:** there are lots of different types of Islamic mortgages (including Ijara, Murabaha and Diminishing Musharaka) that include paying your lender rent or having them co-invest in your property, where you'll buy them out over time. Typically you'll need a higher deposit and it'll cost more over the life of the mortgage, but they're a useful path to homeownership without paying interest.

Mortgage rates

In the UK, interest rates are influenced by the Bank of England, which sets what's known as the 'base rate' (see the 'Strategies for saving' chapter). The Bank of England sometimes changes the base rate to help control inflation and stabilise the economy. Mortgage rates are also linked to the base rate, so you might need to pay particular attention to this depending on the type of mortgage you have. Let's take a look.

Fixed rates

If you choose a fixed-rate mortgage, this means for a period of time, normally between two and five years, your interest rate won't change – it's fixed in place. So even if the base rate goes up or down, your interest rate (and therefore your monthly repayments) will stay the same. When this period ends, you'll normally move on to your lender's 'standard variable rate' (or follow-on rate) if you do nothing. This is typically much higher and can cost hundreds of pounds more per month. Unless you've got a good reason to go on to a standard variable rate – for example, you're in the process of selling up and moving, and don't want to tie yourself into a new deal – it's a good idea to plan ahead and find a new deal.

Variable rates

This means your interest rate (and therefore your monthly repayments) can change in line with the base rate. They're less common as most people prefer to have certainty over how much they're going to pay each month.

Variable rates have various sub-types, including:

- **Discounted rates:** this is where lenders offer a discount on their standard variable rate, normally for two or five years.
- **Tracker rates:** unlike some other variable rate mortgages, where the lender sets their own variable rate, this type of mortgage 'tracks' a reference rate (normally the base rate, or a similar rate set by the lender). So whatever percentage the base rate goes up or down by, your mortgage rate goes up or down by the same amount. These deals usually last between two to five years, but some lenders offer tracker mortgages that last for the whole term of your mortgage, or until you switch to a different deal.

Step 5: get a (realistic!) mortgage in principle

Once you – or your broker – has worked out your affordability, you can apply for what's known as a 'mortgage in principle'.

This is a non-binding offer from a mortgage lender that tells you how much they're willing to lend you. The non-binding part is important here: you might not get exactly the same deal with your *actual* mortgage. But it's really worth doing as it'll give you a clearer sense of what you can afford. Plus, some estate agents and sellers favour those who have one because it can make offers move more quickly, and shows that you're a credible buyer. In fact, in cities like London, where the housing market is more competitive than the Olympics, some estate agents won't even let you view a property without one!

When applying, it's important to be realistic. While it may be tempting to aim for the largest mortgage you qualify for, you'll want to make sure you can comfortably afford the monthly repayments while having money left over to enjoy life (applying the 50–30–20 rule from chapter 4 could be helpful here). How much you're willing to stretch is a personal decision, but try to think longer term and ask yourself questions like:

- Is your income likely to increase or drop in the future?
- Are you expecting a lump sum of money, like an annual bonus?
- Are your outgoings likely to increase? For example, if you've had a baby and need to factor in childcare costs.

Must have

Nice to have

FINDING A PROPERTY

	Must have	Nice to have
Near good schools	☐	☐
Close to train station	☐	☐
Parking or garage	☐	☐
Near to parents	☐	☐
Two bedrooms	☐	☐
One friendly ghost	☐	☐
Garden	☐	☐
Infinity pool & a hot tub	☐	☐

Buying

Finding a property

Browsing on Rightmove is practically a national pastime (the site gets more than 1 million hits *a day*).[5] It's pretty normal to have a dozen tabs open for houses you'll never be able to afford in cities you'll never live in. But once it's time to turn the fantasy into a reality, you'll need to get serious about what you're after. It's rare you'll find a place that ticks every box, so it's good to ask yourself what's essential and what you're happy to be flexible on. Some people create a table of 'must haves' and 'nice to haves' to help them weigh things up. A lot of these factors will likely be influenced by your family, pets, friends and job – not just now, but in the future, too. You might not have children yet but may want a house that'll allow space for it in the next few years. Moving house is expensive, so it's worth figuring out what you need in the long haul.

Is it freehold or leasehold?

If you're thinking about buying a property, you'll need to find out whether it's freehold or leasehold.

Freehold means you own the property itself, so you're the one who's responsible for the upkeep and repairs. In Scotland, the closest equivalent is called a *heritable interest*.

Leasehold means instead of owning the property, you own a lease. At the end of a lease, the property then reverts to whoever granted it (otherwise known as the *freeholder*). The terms of the lease agreement are really important as they determine who's responsible for what. For example, a lease agreement might say you have to get permission to make certain updates to your home, or it might mean the freeholder is responsible for some of the upkeep. As a leaseholder, you may also have to pay service charges or ground rent. A group of leaseholders living in the same building sometimes have a right to jointly buy the freehold of the building or take over its management. Flats are much more likely to be leasehold properties, although houses can be, too. If you're buying a leasehold, a solicitor will be able to tell you what this means for you. It's also worth visiting the government website as leasehold properties are a hot topic and things are always changing, with acts coming into play that are designed to strengthen leaseholders' rights.

Here are some things you'll need to look into if you're buying a leasehold property:

- **The length of the lease:** generally speaking, the longer the lease, the better. While 80 years might sound like a long time, anything below this is usually considered short. Shorter leases lose value more quickly, and extending one can cost a lot of time and money. If you're worried, chat to your solicitor and get their advice.

- **If it has a sinking fund:** try to find out if the other leaseholders have managed to build up a 'sinking fund' – this is a pot of money (usually saved up over a long period of time) that is set aside for major works. Having a sinking fund can help leaseholders plan big expenses in advance.

- **If the fees seem reasonable:** try to find out if the service charge and ground rent seem fair compared to similar homes in the area. Also look out for potential red flags, like service charges that have increased massively from one year to the next.

Making an offer

You've viewed more than 60 places. You've seen and rejected the flat the size of a submarine bunk, and the one with the kitchen in the attic. Now you've found *the one*. It's time to make an offer.

You don't have to go in at the asking price. You can offer less if, for example, you think the property needs repairs that'll cost you a significant amount of money. Or if you think there's a better deal to be had – for instance, if you know that similar properties in the area have sold for less in the same year.

You could find yourself in a competitive scenario where lots of people are offering on the same property. If this happens, the estate agent might invite 'sealed bids', where they'll give you a date and time to make your best and final offer. It's mysterious, dramatic and nerve-racking, with lots of second guessing and uncertainty involved. Just make sure you're comfortable with what you're offering, and don't get too swept up in the urgency – you don't want that initial excitement to evaporate after realising you've stretched yourself too far.

And remember, if one side gets cold feet, they can back out quite easily before contracts are exchanged. This can mean losing some money – for example, you may have already paid out for a solicitor. You might want to consider getting home buyers protection insurance, which can help you claim back some of the fees you've incurred if a sale does fall through. Things are a little different in Scotland, where people are committed to their sale much earlier in the process.

Offer accepted!

The cost of buying

Actually buying your new property is a lengthy process that involves lots of people and paperwork (so much paperwork!). Some of these things can be done all at once, but usually it goes like this:

1. **Instruct a solicitor:** although you can choose to handle the paperwork yourself, it's generally not recommended! Buying a property can be complicated and stressful, so a lot of people call in the professionals and use a solicitor or licensed conveyancer. Most mortgage lenders will have a list of approved solicitors they work with, and your friends might have recommendations, too. Fees vary but they typically range from £800 to £2,500, depending on the value of the property.

2. **Mortgage application:** it's time to apply for a mortgage. If you're working with a broker, they'll handle this for you (see, told you they were great). They might look at the lender you got your mortgage in principle from, or

shop around for a better deal. Applications typically take around two to four weeks for lenders to approve, once they've completed your valuation.

3. **Valuation:** the mortgage lender needs to make sure that the property is worth the amount you've offered. This protects them in case you ever stop paying your mortgage and they need to repossess and sell your home – basically they have to make sure they could recover their money, if it ever came to that. Most lenders won't charge extra for a valuation, but if they do, it typically costs around £150 to £500, depending on the value of the property.

4. **Survey:** you don't have to get a survey, but it's a good idea if you want to be nice and thorough. This is where an independent professional checks the property for things like structural problems that could impact the property's value. The results can help you work out the cost of fixing any issues, which might make you decide to negotiate a lower offer, or even pull out altogether. For example, if the roof needed replacing, you could get quotes for the work and knock this amount off your offer. Prices vary by quite a bit, as you can pick different 'levels' of survey – the more thorough, the more expensive.

5. **Enquiries:** if you're buying a home in England and Wales, there's a (very formal and ever-so-slightly spooky sounding) principle known as 'let the buyer beware'. This means it's on you to find out everything you want

or need to know before you buy. It doesn't mean you have to stake the place out in head-to-toe blackout gear, just that your solicitor will ask the seller to fill in quite a long questionnaire. But just bear in mind that ultimately it's your responsibility to make sure you're happy with the property before going through with the purchase. If you discover something worrying later on (like a legal dispute), it's usually on you to deal with it unless the seller deliberately misled you.

6. **Searches:** carried out by your solicitor or conveyancer, these are essentially checks on the property and surrounding area. They look for things like planning restrictions and flood risks. This is to make sure that everything looks above board before you finalise the purchase.

7. **Exchange contracts:** your solicitor will prepare draft contracts – one for you and one for the seller. Once everyone's happy with the terms, you'll both sign and exchange contracts. At exchange of contracts, you'll pay your deposit and finalise your mortgage; confirming the amount you're borrowing and telling your lender when you plan to 'complete'. This is the equally scary and exciting point of no return! If you pull out after exchanging, you'll be in breach of contract and the seller will have the right to keep your deposit and sell to someone else. So before exchanging contracts, it's really important to be sure.

8. **Complete:** this is a *huge* milestone day. It's when you pay the remaining balance of the property price, which normally comes from both your deposit and the help of a mortgage, and ownership officially transfers to you. On completion day, you'll get the keys to your new kingdom!

9. **Move-in day and takeaway:** at long last, it's the moment you've been waiting for. Move-in day has finally arrived and it's time to haul your things from wherever they've been lurking (a storage unit, your parents' garage, or the rented flat where you last assembled IKEA furniture at 2am) into your new place. Even if you're strong enough for an impromptu weightlifting session, consider hiring professional movers if your budget allows as it can save you a lot of energy – and possibly a few friendships. Of course, you *could* make a Pot Noodle for dinner (that is, if you can find your kettle), but it's tradition to sit on the floor and eat a takeaway to celebrate your brand new home.

Case study

'We're buying a house together but what happens if we split up?'

Amman and Caroline are both accountants in their 30s who live with their cockapoos, Cleo and Haiku. They're in the process of buying their first home together – a two-bed terraced house in Exeter for £280,000. They have a combined income of £85,000, and £40,000 in savings for their deposit. Amman has saved £19,000 and inherited £5,000 from his aunt, and Caroline has saved £16,000.

The first big decision their solicitor asked them to make was how they wanted to own the property: as joint tenants or tenants in common. Since they were contributing different amounts to the deposit, their solicitor advised them to go in as tenants in common. This would help protect their individual contributions in case they ever broke up. At first they found it a bit cynical to think that way, but after they read more about tenants in common online, they decided it was a smart thing to do.

Next up, Amman and Caroline had to get their mortgage application approved, which involved a huge pile of paperwork and approximately 97 emails. They had a mortgage adviser, who made a list of all the documents they had to collate: six months' worth of bank statements, payslips, proof of their deposit, and details of their monthly outgoings. Around two weeks later, their mortgage was approved. They got a 25-year term at a fixed rate for the first five years.

Once it was time to exchange contracts, Amman and Caroline paid the deposit to their solicitor. It was both thrilling and terrifying to see their savings leave their account! Completion followed three weeks later, and they celebrated over dinner at their new local.

Even though they contributed different amounts to

the deposit, Amman and Caroline decided to split the monthly mortgage repayments equally. They earned similar salaries and were planning to jointly contribute to the household expenses, so it felt like the fairest way. Their monthly mortgage repayment was £1,200, so they each paid £600 into a joint account along with extra cash for things like household bills, contents insurance and endless paint tester pots.

At the suggestion of their solicitor, they documented their tenants in common set-up with a Declaration of Trust (also known as a Deed of Trust), which cost them £300 to have drawn up. This is a legally binding document that specified:

- The 60/40 split in property ownership
- Their equal contributions to the monthly mortgage repayments
- How the proceeds would be divided if they sold the house
- Their agreement that in case of a sale, Amman would get his bigger deposit back

Their solicitor also helped them draw up a will so they could ensure their house share and other assets would be shared out according to their wishes if the worst happened.

Even though Amman and Caroline are in a trusting, long-term relationship, they knew it was sensible to document the deposit split to avoid any future disputes or stress.

I own a home. Now what?

You're on the ladder! And once you're on, it can be easier to keep climbing. For example, if you want to climb up, you might be able to use the equity in your current home towards the deposit for your next one. Or if you're thinking about climbing down – say, downsizing or moving to a cheaper area – you might have more options, since you won't have to borrow as much. Of course, this all depends on the state of the housing market and your overall financial situation.

Once you're in your new home, there'll be some financial responsibilities that, for first-time buyers especially, can take some getting used to. Things like . . .

- **Insurance:** most lenders require buildings insurance as part of the mortgage terms, as it protects the value of the property. This type of insurance covers the structure of the building – things like the roof, floors, windows and built-in fixtures like bathrooms. Even if you own your property outright, it's a good idea to have this cover to protect you against things like fires, floods and storm damage. Good news for leaseholders – your freeholder is normally responsible for this cost. You might want to look into contents insurance at this point, too.
- **Renovation costs:** buying a 'doer upper' can be a more affordable way to get on the property ladder. But of course, remodelling doesn't come for free, so it's

worth balancing how much you plan to spend with the potential resale value of your home. For example, if you spend £10,000 on a shiny new kitchen with a built-in wine fridge, is it likely you'll make this money back when you come to sell? The longer you stay in a property, the less of an issue this is, as houses tend to appreciate in value over time. But if you're only there for a couple of years, it might not make financial sense to plough lots of money into it. That said, a property's not just a financial investment, it's an emotional one. Investing money into it simply to make it feel like home is totally valid.

- **Maintenance and repairs:** when you own your home, your safety net will be more important than ever. You're effectively your own landlord now, so you're responsible for fixing things like broken boilers and leaky taps.
- **Service charges:** if you live in a leasehold property, you might have to pay an annual service charge to cover cleaning and maintenance of shared areas like grounds and communal hallways. You should be made aware of this during the buying process (way before contracts are exchanged) but even so, it can take a little getting used to if you've never had this kind of outgoing before.

To overpay, or not to overpay?

Your monthly mortgage repayments are worked out so that, by the end of the full term, you'll have repaid the loan and interest (if you've chosen a repayment mortgage). But you can choose to *overpay* your mortgage by paying off a lump

FLAT OUT LEGAL
KEEPING PROPERTY DEALS MOVING

'I worked out that if I overpay my mortgage,
I could save £45,000 in interest.'

Ellis, 37, is a carpenter from Portsmouth.

To buy his first flat, he got a **£200,000 mortgage** over
a **35-year term.** He opted into a five-year fixed deal with
a **4.5% interest rate.** His monthly payment was **£950.**

A year after moving in, Ellis got a pay rise which gave him
roughly **£100 extra a month.** He already had his budgeting
down to a fine art, and knew that he didn't need the extra
money to put towards any of his essential outgoings.
He thought about putting it into a high-interest savings
account, until one of his colleagues told him about
mortgage overpayments.

Ellis put the numbers into a mortgage calculator, and
found that if he overpaid by **£100 a month,** he could save
a whopping **£45,000 in interest,** and be mortgage-free
seven years earlier.

He was shocked at how these relatively small
overpayments could have such a big impact on his
mortgage. Seeing how this would benefit him in the
future gave Ellis the motivation to go for it.

sum or paying higher monthly amounts. Just keep in mind that most mortgages only allow you to overpay 10% before hitting you with hefty early repayment charges.

It can be really motivating to track how much of the house you actually own, as your share increases and the bank's gets smaller. It's even more motivating when you start to calculate *overpayments* – showing you how much you could save on interest, and how much earlier you could become mortgage-free.

Buying a property is one of the biggest and most emotional purchases you are ever likely to make. From the positive emotions that come with having an offer accepted (excitement, joy, relief) to the mixed emotions associated with seeing your deposit finally leave your account (more excitement, more relief, complete terror). Simply put, a home is one of the very few purchases in life that engages both your brain and your heart in such a meaningful way.

The Deeded Dish

110895 Treasury Terrace,
Goldenfields, GF9 2XP, United Kingdom

TAKEAWAYS

ITEM	QTY
Give your finances a spring clean	1
Budget for the extras	1
Don't give up	1
TOTAL	**3**

HAVE A NICE DAY

TAKEAWAYS

Give your finances a spring clean: in the lead-up to applying for a mortgage, give yourself time to balance your budget, repay any high-interest debt and sort out all the paperwork you need. It'll save you a lot of time down the line.

Budget for the extras: when you're buying, you're so focused on the big costs – like your deposit and Stamp Duty – it can be easy to forget the smaller ones, like hiring a removal firm or getting a survey done. Buying a place always costs more than you think it will, and while an unexpected bill of £200 might not sound like a huge deal today, it can feel monumental when you're in the middle of a property purchase. Try setting up a pot for additional expenses to avoid being caught out.

Don't give up: almost a third of house purchases fall through before completion.[6] While it can be really disheartening, if you're serious about buying somewhere, you'll need to strengthen that mental muscle that allows you to dust yourself off and keep going. And on the bright side, setbacks can actually make you a savvier buyer who knows what red flags to look out for next time.

Chapter 11
Keeping your money safe

You might think the British drive on the left just to be difficult, but it's actually a tradition that dates back to the Middle
Ages. Back then, people travelled down dark country roads
and lived in fear of thieves lurking in the bushes. You had to
be ready for anything and if you were right-handed, like most
people, riding on the left meant you could draw your sword
to defend yourself. Swap a noble steed for a Lime bike and
a sack of gold coins for an iPhone 17, and you'll find that not
much has changed. Crime is as old as the hills, and fraud is
no different. But as times change, so do the methods criminals use to get at your valuables. Now, the vast majority of
money is electronic – only 4% of it exists in physical cash.[1]
Criminals will always go where the money is, which means
you're more likely to come across them online than down a
dark country road.

The internet can be a pretty great place. After all, it's
where videos of skateboarding dogs live. But it also makes

it much harder to know who to trust, and much easier for scammers to stay anonymous. The digital platforms and online shops that make life easier also create endless opportunities for scammers to get at your money. You can put a name and face to a person in real life, but on the internet identities can be invented in seconds. Fraudsters are always looking out for new opportunities to gain and exploit people's trust, and nobody wants to think they're naive enough to fall for a scam. Plus, there are common misconceptions around what a victim of fraud might look like – maybe you picture someone older and not as internet-savvy. But it's this perception, along with the sophisticated tactics scammers use, that helped make fraud the number one reported crime in 2024.[2] The unfortunate and uncomfortable truth is that *anyone* can experience fraud, so everyone should be prepared for it. Because once you are, you can get back to watching videos of dogs doing silly things with total peace of mind.

It's impossible to list every scam, so we'll break down the main kinds you might come across, share some of the most common examples and show you how to stay vigilant. And we'll keep coming back to trust, because every scam or attempt to steal your money relies on exploiting it. That doesn't mean you should live in fear and trust no one – only that being wary can help save you time, money and stress down the line.

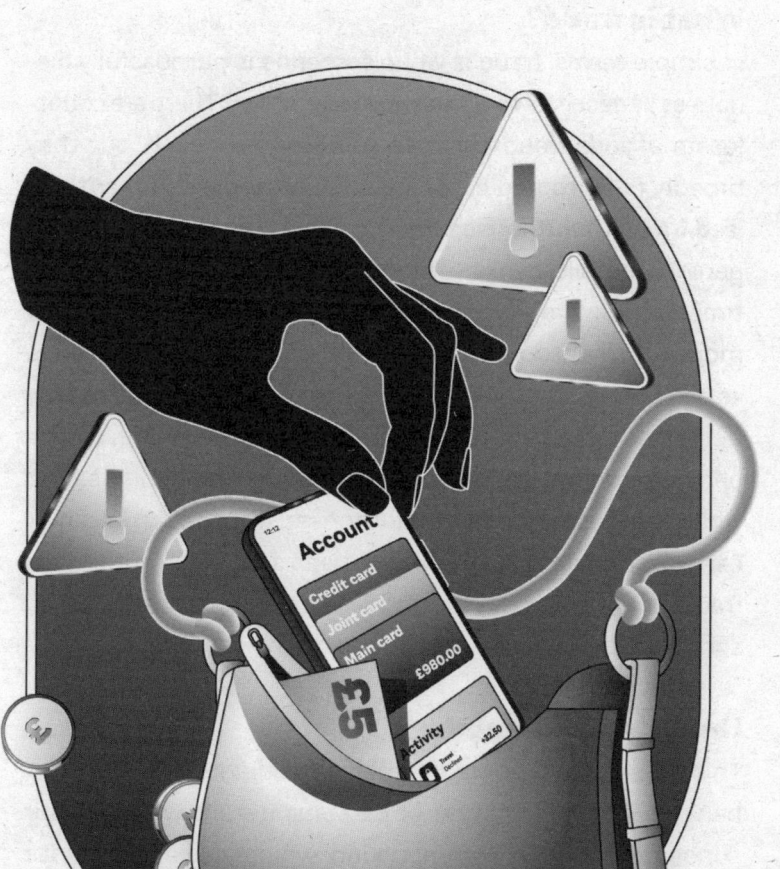

What is fraud?

In simple terms, fraud is when someone is purposefully dishonest or deceitful to try to steal your money. There are countless methods fraudsters use to swipe your cash, but they broadly fall into two categories: unauthorised and authorised fraud. *Unauthorised fraud* is when someone steals your personal details, banking information, cards or phone, sometimes without you even realising, and uses them to take your money. *Authorised fraud* is what you might typically describe as a scam – when you're tricked into giving someone money by making a payment to them yourself. This generally happens because you believe they're trustworthy and genuine. And while you'll usually catch unauthorised fraud fairly quickly, it can take a while to realise you've been a victim of authorised fraud, sometimes even months. Let's dig into how you can spot both types, and what you can do to keep safe.

Unauthorised fraud

This type of fraud is clear-cut theft – fraudsters take your card, banking app information or personal details without your consent. The most common kind, which also accounts for the highest losses, is someone stealing your card or details.[3] Criminals are always inventing new ways to get at your cash or banking details, but generally they fall into these buckets:

- **Stealing your login details:** when a fraudster uses your login details or information to access your online banking. They can get these by stealing your phone while it's unlocked, or by calling you and tricking you into believing they're your bank and need access to your account to help 'protect' your money. These calls can be really deceptive, with criminal cold callers going as far as googling real staff members at your bank to impersonate them, then asking you convincing sounding security questions to get your card details, password or PIN and steal your money. Because it's so convincing, nearly 43 million adults in the UK have fallen victim, with one in five left more than £1,000 out of pocket.[4]

- **Fake text messages or emails, AKA 'phishing':** criminals use text messages and emails to bait you into clicking on dodgy links to legit-looking websites, to get you to give away personal information. They might seem like the real deal, but once you click through and enter your details, they steal them. The information they take could be anything from your bank details to your email address and passwords. Once scammers have your passwords, they can change them and lock you out of your accounts – draining your bank account or buying things online. Be especially careful if you get messages about car accident claims or missed package deliveries! Think before you click, and use your common sense; have you actually been in an accident and are you even waiting for a package?

- **Hacking company data:** this is when a company you've shopped with or have an account with loses your data. Criminals can get access to information like your card details, which can end up leading to identity theft. Here's an example: in April 2018, we received reports of fraud from around 50 customers and spotted that around 70% of them had used Ticketmaster – an unusually high proportion. Ticketmaster later told us they'd been hacked and criminals had stolen their customers' card details. Fortunately, we caught it early and took steps to reduce the risk of customers losing a lot of money.

- **Identity theft:** this is when criminals pretend to be you – using your details to apply for things like loans, credit cards, mobile phone contracts and bank accounts. Aside from the stress and upset this causes, it can also quickly damage your credit score. To spot identity theft, look out for things like letters from solicitors, bailiffs, or debt collectors about debts you don't recognise. Or if you apply for a loan or credit card and it gets denied, this could be a clue that your credit score is lower than you thought, possibly due to fraud. So keep an eye on your credit score, and look into it if it suddenly drops and you can't think why. To keep yourself doubly safe, you could also get identity theft insurance, which helps cover the related costs, like any legal expenses and recovering the stolen money.

How to stay safe

Your older siblings were on to something when they asked you for a top-secret password to enter their fort. When it comes to protecting your money, it really does pay to play it safe. Here are three ways to protect yourself from having your details stolen:

- **Always take your time:** before you click a link or share your details over the phone, always take a beat to ask yourself if things seem legitimate. Were you expecting the call or message? Do you definitely trust what's being asked of you, or who's asking it? How does the request make you feel in the moment? Never be rushed into anything. And remember, your bank is actually unlikely to ever call you. But if they do and you weren't expecting it, hang up and ring them back on their registered phone number. Some banks are also covered by the 159 hotline, an emergency number you can call to report financial scams as they happen. When you dial 159, they'll ask you for the name of your bank and connect you to them.

- **Protect your details when you're out and about:** less screen time is never a bad thing, and less screen time when you're out and about is just plain smart! Leaving your phone unlocked or getting it out in public where someone could snatch it means thieves could gain access to your email account. And once they're in, they can change your password and gain access to *other* accounts, since a lot of them use email verification. You can imagine how this can spiral very quickly, with criminals suddenly gaining access to your bank account. You can add an additional layer of protection to your phone by switching on two-step verification. This is when you need both a password and a second type of identification like a text message with a code, or your fingerprint, face or retina on a smartphone.

- **Protect your details online:** there are lots of ways to protect your details online. First and foremost, use a password manager. They make life easier by creating, saving and auto-filling strong passwords for you, so you don't need to remember them. They even scramble your passwords, so if a hacker does get in, they can't see them. Only *you* can unlock everything with a special master password. And be extremely careful where you put sensitive information like your date of birth, phone number or answers to common security questions (like your dog's name or where you went to school). It might sound obvious but it's easy to innocently post stuff on social media that could provide clues. Also consider deleting your physical card details from checkout presets and using a virtual card instead. These let you buy things online without sharing your regular card details. If you think someone's got hold of the virtual card details, you can delete it and create a new one.

- **Keep an eye out:** just as important as understanding where your money goes, is knowing where it *shouldn't* go. Pay attention to your transactions, turn on notifications, and tell your bank straight away if something looks wrong.

'I can't believe someone guessed my 1234 PIN'

More than 80% of accounts are hacked because of stolen, weak or reused passwords. Here are the most easy-to-hack passwords people used in the UK in 2024 . . .[5]

1. password
2. qwerty123
3. qwerty1
4. 123456
5. liverpool

6. 123456789
7. password1
8. qwerty
9. arsenal
10. 12345678

If you're guilty of using any of these, this is your reminder to change them!

Authorised fraud, or scams

Rather than stealing your cash or details directly, criminals deceive or manipulate you into trusting them, so you hand your money over willingly. These scams can be slow burns that criminals nurture over a long period of time to build up your trust and lower your defences, which makes falling victim especially difficult to process. Victims often feel shame and denial, because nobody wants to believe they'd hand over their hard-earned money 'willingly'. But scammers are clever and convincing, and this type of fraud is becoming really common.[6] The antidote? Extra caution and slowing things down. If a request feels ridiculously time-sensitive, unusual, surprising or confusing, it's worth taking a moment before acting on it. And if something seems too good to be true, it probably is. So always take some time to reflect on how you feel, ask yourself if something seems off, and even chat to friends and tell them what's happening. After all, if it is a scam, they might've heard about it or experienced something similar themselves.

There are endless scams out there and they're constantly evolving. But they always prey on our emotions and instincts to gain trust and seem believable, which is why they fall into a few different patterns or types:

- **When you buy something that doesn't exist:** is there anything better than scoring an amazing deal on something you really want? Especially if money's a bit tight, or you're trying to stick to a budget. Fraudsters take advantage of this, using a combination of tactics to trick you into buying something that isn't real. More than 80% of these scams take place on social platforms like Facebook Marketplace, with scammers tapping into big cultural moments like gigs because they have huge resale markets and loyal fanbases willing to part with their cash.[7] Criminals also keep track of trends and change their tactics throughout the year, offering 'unmissable' deals on things like holidays, Christmas gifts or those sold-out trainers you know you'll look great in. As well as fake items, you should also look out for entirely fake websites. Scammers often use ads on social media to promote them, which unsuspecting shoppers click on. Some fake websites can be incredibly slick and convincing, with professional-looking photography and Ts and Cs. So even if a site looks the part, it's best not to make assumptions. Use a safe browsing tool – an add-on that filters websites and files for malware – and think twice about how you landed on the website. Did you type in the URL yourself, or follow a potentially dodgy link?

The pitfalls of buying and selling online

Clothes, furniture, artwork, books about money – there's no limit to what you can buy and sell online. And there's also no limit to the amount of scams that are designed to catch you out. Here are the two most common ones to watch out for.

The PayPal overpayment scam, which is when a scammer buys something from you and 'accidentally' pays too much. For example, you sell them a pair of shoes and they pay you £20 extra. They'll say it was a mistake and ask you to refund the £20. They'll usually ask you to send this refund to a different account than the one they paid you from. That's because the original payment they sent you is often from a stolen account, and will eventually be reversed by the real account holder's bank. This leaves you without the shoes, as you've sent them, *and* out of pocket for the money you refunded.

The proof of postage scam is when you sell something – like that VR headset you never use – and a fraudster asks to pay you via bank transfer. You get an email that looks like it's from a bank, claiming the buyer has sent you the cash, which they'll release as soon as you provide proof you've sent the item. The email's designed to look legit, using real bank logos and formatting. The idea is that you'll trust what you're reading and post the item. But because the email is fake, the 'buyer' never transferred any money to your account. The scammer now has the item, and hasn't paid you for it.

- **When scammers pretend to be a company you trust –** like your bank or HMRC – to manipulate you into sharing details or sending them money. Usually the scammer will have information about you, like your name, address or card number, and use them to quickly build trust that they are who they say they are. They might even be smart about *when* they contact you, for example, by getting in touch around the time your tax return is due. If someone contacts you by phone, you should hang up and call the number on the organisation's website. If someone contacts you by email or letter, look out for giveaways like typos, strange grammar and unofficial-looking email addresses or letter heads. That said, these scams can be really convincing – scammers will often use AI to reduce these kinds of errors and make their correspondence look super professional. So always get in touch with your bank or HMRC if you're unsure whether something's legit.

- **When scammers pretend to be a family member:** by sending a text or WhatsApp, usually opening with a generic, seemingly innocent 'Hello Mum' or 'Hi mate'. The scammer will then go on to claim they urgently need money and ask you to transfer it to them. This type of scam can look like it's from your friend's actual phone number, as criminals might have stolen their phone or can easily mimic their number. Whichever number it comes from, think about how they'd usually speak to you, and be wary if anything seems odd, like your 15-year-old suddenly saying 'Can you urgently transfer me £100 please?' instead of 'Mum, can I have 10 quid?' If you don't give in right away, the messages usually become more urgent and pushy, which can often be when you realise the scammer isn't who they say they are. Also be aware that the scammer's relying on you giving them information to fill in the blanks – for example, if you reply with a name, that gives them information they didn't already have. If you're not sure, call them or ask them a question only they'd know the answer to.

- **When you invest in something that doesn't exist:** this is when someone uses a cold call, message or advert to trick you into making a fake investment. You might think these scams always make ridiculous promises about the returns you could make, and many do. But our research shows that some fraudsters are actually very careful to make sure the scam doesn't look too good to be true.[8] Sometimes, victims might see an initial return on their investment, and even have the freedom to make withdrawals. They might also add you to a group chat on WhatsApp with other supposed 'investors' taking part in the scheme, and share fake graphs or data. All of these things create the illusion you're in control, and convince you that everything's above board – again, building trust over time. The fraudsters will then start charging you fake insurance and withdrawal fees, and after that your money will disappear. They might also ask you to open an account with a crypto firm as part of this scam, and to send them crypto so they can invest it for you.

Remember, if you're being asked to do something you're uncomfortable with, *especially* if it involves opening a new account somewhere, be cautious.

When we spoke to customers who'd fallen victim to investment scams, we found that they broadly fell into two groups: those who were driven by *hope* (they saw money as a way out of tough situations), and those who were driven by *comfort* (they saw money as a path to financial freedom). Those driven by hope were targeted because they were vulnerable – as an example, some of them hadn't been in the UK for very long. They were targeted on social media, with promises from seemingly friendly experts. Those who were driven by comfort tended to be scam-aware and cautious, so they might seem like less obvious targets. In reality, because they considered themselves savvy enough not to make a mistake, they got caught up in bigger schemes that promised bigger returns, and were lured by false recommendations and reviews from people who were 'like them'. The bottom line is that anyone can be caught out, and there's no such thing as a 'typical' victim.

To keep yourself safe when investing, watch out for red flags like investment schemes that seem complicated, hold assets that aren't related to real companies or things, or involve transferring money abroad. Flip back to the 'Becoming an investor' chapter for more information.

- **When you pay a deposit for something you never receive:** this is when you're asked for money upfront in return for a larger chunk of money. It's not an investment (where you're expecting a percentage return on something) but a small initial payment that promises you a much larger payment in return. Some examples of this include loan fee fraud, where you pay an initial 'deposit' expecting to receive a loan in return, but actually end up being charged more fictitious fees and insurance costs. Another example is a job task scam, where you think you're being recruited into a remote online job. To receive your salary, the scammer will ask you to put a little bit of money into an account (usually crypto). They'll get you to add more and more top-ups into this account to cover fake fees or negative balances. Then unsurprisingly, your 'salary' never materialises.

- **When scammers pose as a love interest:** when it comes to online dating, you might think the only thing to watch out for is someone lying about their height or liking pineapple on pizza. But criminals rely on romantic connections forged online to run some of the longest scams going! They usually start by 'love bombing' their victim – saying they love you after only a few days or weeks of talking, or sharing incredibly personal stories with you. Basically, doing anything to try to build a sense of trust and intimacy very quickly. Once you trust them, they start asking you for money, often to support their career, or let them travel to you, or because they've had an emergency and need help. While you might speak on the phone with them, you'll very rarely meet them in person. It can sometimes take years for a romance scam to come to light, as more often than not, you develop real feelings for this person and don't want to believe they could be deceiving you. The 'Tinder Swindler' is probably the most famous example of this. Made into a smash Netflix documentary, a man posed as a wealthy diamond dealer on a dating app, and then stole from the women he met by claiming he was in danger and urgently needed money. In some cases, scammers might even pose as celebrities and scour social media fan pages to find innocent people to exploit.

Case study

'I wish I'd listened to my gut instead of ignoring the red flags.'

Sheona, 43, is renovating her flat, and things are getting expensive. Who knew doorknobs cost so much? She's been shopping around, trying to find herself some bargains, and has successfully scored a few deals on resell sites like eBay and Facebook Marketplace, always being careful to read seller reviews before committing.

To celebrate reaching a big milestone – she finally finished her living room! – Sheona decided to treat herself to a new smart TV. It'll be so nice to have her friends over for movie nights again.

She visits a few well-known websites she's shopped with before, but they're all so expensive. A few days later, an ad pops up while she's browsing online, showing her an electronics company she's not heard of before. She clicks on the link and lands on a slick-looking site. At the bottom of the homepage, she spots a row of glowing customer reviews. She browses around the site and after a couple of minutes, she sees the TV she's been eying up – and it's on sale! The webpage says there are only two TVs left and the sale price is for a limited time only, so she quickly adds it to her basket so she doesn't miss out. She starts typing in her bank details but then hesitates . . . There's a little voice in her head asking: *but why is this so cheap? Seems weird, Sheona!*

She does a quick Google search on the company and finds more glowing testimonials on an independent review site. Something seems odd, though – nearly all of them were written within the last week or so. She pings a message in her 'Broke but optimistic club' WhatsApp group and asks her friends what they think.

She hesitates for a moment and then thinks she's being silly – after all, how could someone fake an entire *website*? Sheona adds her debit card details and hits the 'pay now' button. Immediately a message pops up saying that the site's card payments aren't working, but the pop-up lists some alternative bank account details she can use to pay. The account name is a bit weird – it's a person's

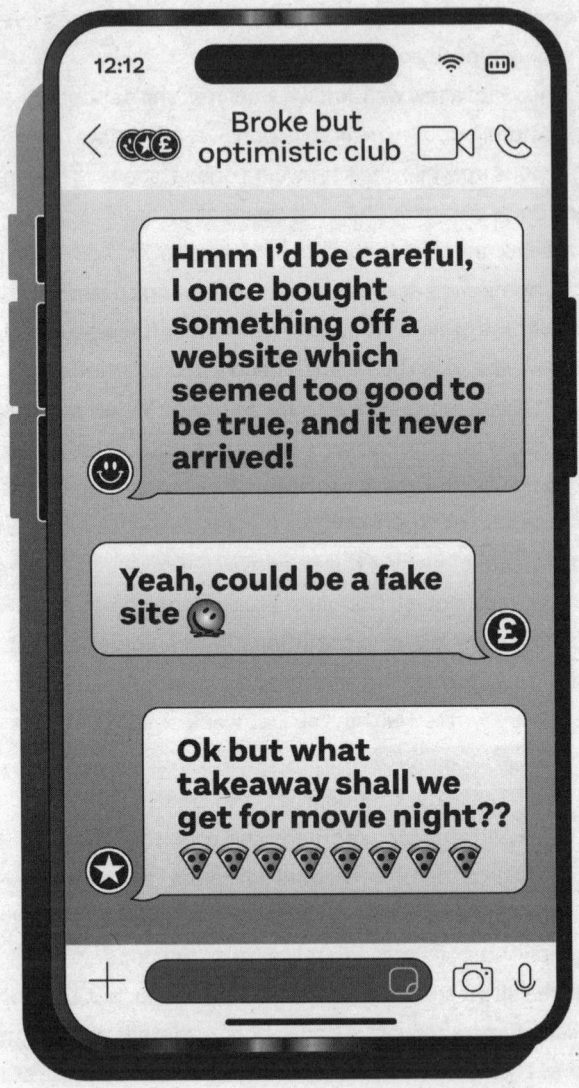

name rather than the name of the site – but she guesses it must just be the person who runs the company. Not wanting to miss out on the great price, she brushes off any concerns, opens her banking app and sends the money. She waits for her confirmation email, but after an hour it still hasn't arrived. Worried now, Sheona looks on the website for contact details and calls the number listed, but it's disconnected. Realising that everything about the situation feels really off, Sheona calls her bank and explains the situation. They assess it as a scam and immediately cancel her card and PIN, and send her a replacement in the post. They also decide to refund her the money she sent and give her some advice on what red flags to look out for in the future.

Sheona's glad her bank acted so quickly, but the whole thing left her feeling really shaken and upset. She's learned a valuable lesson, though, even if it means she won't be watching *The Traitors* in Ultra HD for now.

Things to do before you send anyone money

Nobody wants to go through life giving everyone the side eye, but caution really is the best defence against scammers. So if you treat every invitation to make a payment or input sensitive information as a potential scam, there's less chance criminals will be successful in their attempts to catch you out. Here are a few things you can do before you part with your money.

- Pay by card instead of bank transfer when you can. Bank transfers aren't protected in the same way as card payments, so once you've sent money to a fraudster, it can be difficult to get it back. A credit card is even safer for purchases over £100 because of something called Section 75 of the Consumer Credit Act, a law that gives you the right to claim a refund from your credit provider if there's a problem with the goods or service.

- If you are paying by bank transfer, pay attention to warnings from your bank that flag if the details you've been given don't match the receiving account, as this could be a sign someone's using a fake name, for example. You can then decide if you trust where the money's going before paying it.

- Buy from trusted merchants whenever you can. But if you are buying from a company you've not used before, always check verified reviews. Just be wary of any write-ups that sound super similar, or multiple reviews written on the same date, as they might not be genuine.

- Don't trust anything that seems too good to be true, like an item that's a lot cheaper than it should be, or an investment that promises large guaranteed returns.

- If it's a company, check it's regulated. From our research, we know most victims of fraud rely on a cursory check of a company's website to decide if something looks legitimate or not, but it's really important to do your due diligence.[9] Check the Financial Conduct Authority (FCA) register for financial services, and for travel companies use ABTA.

Will I get my money back?

Discovering someone has stolen from you is a truly horrible feeling, and nobody wants to find themselves in that position. But the good news is, if you're a victim of *unauthorised fraud*, your bank is usually required to repay you the money you lost. And if you catch someone draining your account in real time, you can try to stop them in their tracks by freezing your card or putting a block on your account. The main thing is to stay calm and, hard as it may feel, try not to panic. Things are a little more complicated when it comes to *authorised fraud*. Banks will look at what happened in each case and decide if they'll reimburse you, following the rules set by the regulator to make sure they're treating victims consistently.

The Financial Conduct Authority (FCA)

The FCA is an independent regulatory body that oversees the UK's financial markets and services, like banks and insurance companies. It sets rules and standards to ensure that financial firms treat their customers fairly, so it's important to make sure your money's held with an FCA-authorised provider.

If you've been a victim of fraud, don't beat yourself up or feel embarrassed. Scammers are becoming ever more sophisticated in their attempts to manipulate our normal human desires to save money, improve our lives, or help the people we love. Being scammed doesn't make you gullible or foolish, it just makes you human. But with some simple precautions and awareness, you can help make sure that you don't fall prey to scammers. Just remember, if it does happen to you, contact your bank, building society or credit card provider immediately. You can also contact Action Fraud, via the police website, and Citizens Advice.

Under Lock & Quiche

41 Treasury Terrace,
Goldenfields, GF9 2XP, United Kingdom

TAKEAWAYS

ITEM	QTY
Protect yourself	1
Proceed with caution	1
Act fast if something happens	1
TOTAL	3

HAVE A NICE DAY

TAKEAWAYS

Protect yourself: being *proactive* is always better than being *reactive*. Put measures in place to make it harder for thieves and scammers to catch you out in the first place. Switch on face or touch ID for your banking apps, keep your phone safe, turn on two-factor authentication, and be careful about what information you share online.

Proceed with caution: always give yourself time to think and trust your gut if something feels off, like you're being rushed into making a payment, or you get a phone call or text that doesn't sound right. It might feel awkward or like a faff to double-check or question things, but you'll always be glad you did if something turns out to be a scam.

Act fast if something happens: call your bank or the 159 hotline immediately if something suspicious happens, like you get a phone call from someone claiming to be them. And if your card or phone is stolen, get in touch with your bank straight away to freeze your account. The sooner you act, the less time a thief or scammer has to do real damage.

Chapter 12
Life after work

Remember when you were a kid and you thought your parents and their friends were ancient? They were actually probably in their 30s or 40s; maybe even younger than you are now. And one day, impossible as it might seem, there will come a time when you'll be *even* older, inching ever closer towards the inevitable . . . retirement!

The thought of old age can conjure up competing images for people. One might be sipping piña coladas on a cruise, and the other might be a little more austere and grey. How you visualise your retirement can be a product of your hopes and fears about the future. It can be overwhelming and scary to think about, with more than a quarter of Gen Zs and millennials saying they're not confident they'll be able to retire comfortably.[1] But if you take the time to plan for it now, retirement can be the best long holiday you ever take. The passport? Your pension.

At a really basic level, your pension is a pot – or pots – you pay money into while you're working. You usually can't touch it until you're in your late 50s, you can't spend it, you probably won't even think about it. Instead, it grows quietly in the background without you noticing. Then, when it's time to hang up your work boots, you take the money out of that pot to live on. How you live will be hugely influenced by how much goes into this pot, but it's also down to other financial decisions you make throughout your life, like whether or not you buy a property, and how much you've saved and invested. If you flip back to the 'Principles for your money' chapter, you'll remember that time is one of your biggest superpowers. That's because the longer you give your money to work for you, the more it should grow. It's a really key principle that comes up in most of the chapters and it's especially important here. Because when it comes to retirement, your spending, saving and investing habits *now* are the things that'll impact your life *later*. It's when you'll rake in all the rewards of those sweet, sweet compound returns you built up over the decades. It may feel abstract to plan so far ahead, but small changes to things like your pension contributions could genuinely mean more beachside sunsets in your sunset years. And who doesn't want that?

Defined contribution versus defined benefit pensions

When we talk about paying into a pension pot that grows over time, we're talking about a common type of private pension known as a 'defined contribution pension'. The money in your pot goes into investments, and how much you have by retirement depends on how well those investments perform.

There's another type known as a 'defined benefit pension' (sometimes called a 'final salary' or 'career average' pension), which is more common if you work in the public sector, like the NHS. Typically you might get a percentage of your final salary when you retire, or sometimes an average of your salary over your career. Because these pensions depend on the rules of your scheme, we won't go into detail about them here. Just be aware that if you have one of these pensions, some of what we'll talk about in this chapter won't apply to you.

Pension procrastination

Although the thought of retirement can be an absolute dream – especially when your alarm's going off at 6am and you have three missed calls from your boss – people still avoid planning for it. Many young people see pensions as a distant worry.[2] After all, when you're living large in your 20s and 30s, a faraway future where you're in worse health and closer to death probably isn't something you want to dwell on! And it doesn't help that the government keeps moving the goalposts. By the end of 2028, the state pension age will rise to 67, then to 68 between 2044 and 2046. When you know you'll be working that long, retirement doesn't feel particularly pressing. But because of the magic of compounding,

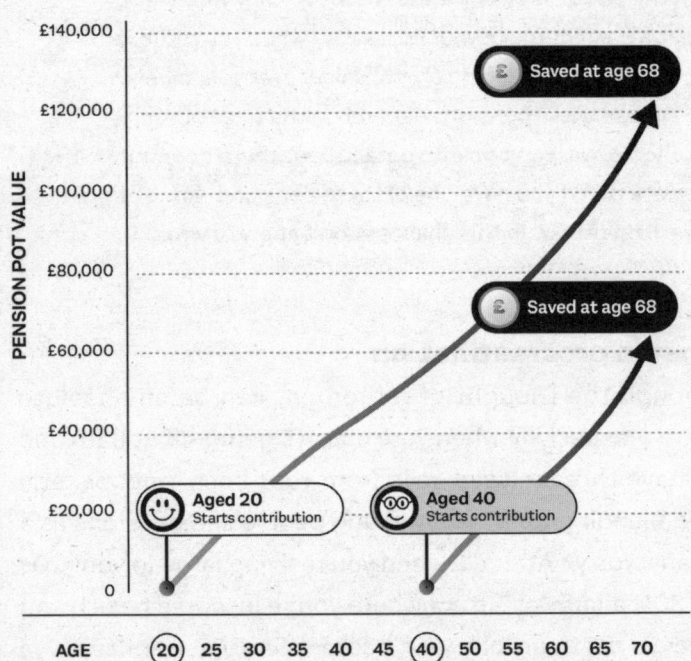

COMPOUNDING ON PENSION

1984 Dividend Drive,
Manchester, M15 4QD, United Kingdom

Thank you! Come again!

*For illustrative purposes only -
remember investments can fall as well as rise
in value and returns aren't guaranteed.*

the earlier you start saving and thinking about retirement, the better.

Pensions are often misunderstood, with 54% of millennials believing that their pension savings earn a fixed amount of interest.[3] But actually, most workplace and private pensions are investments. Remember the stock market we talked about in the 'Becoming an Investor' chapter? A large chunk of your pension is likely to be invested there, and made up of a range of investment types, like bonds, cash, commodities, company shares and property. This means your money should grow, but the value will go up and down over time, and the final value isn't guaranteed. Depending on your pension provider, you can control what fund your pension invests in. And just like the other types of investments we covered in chapter 8, you can choose the level of risk you're comfortable taking.

Case study

'A pension didn't feel like a priority for me, until I did the maths.'

Emily is a 22-year-old university graduate from Essex.

After four years of studying and work placements, she's just been offered her first full-time role as a veterinary nurse. Her parents have stressed the importance of making the most of her workplace pension, but she's considering opting out as she'd rather have more in her pocket to enjoy now. To help her see the power of compound returns, her parents helped her work out how much she could end up with if she started now, compared to if she delayed the decision.

They based their sums on the following figures:

Annual salary: £30,000
Annual salary increase: 2%
Employer contribution: 5%
Emily's contribution: 3%
Investment growth rate: inflation + 5%*
Withdrawal rate in retirement: 4% per year
Retirement age: 68

Here's a breakdown based on these figures, and assuming an average life expectancy of 89 years:[4]

Scenario 1: If Emily starts her workplace pension at 22:
- Emily contributes **8% of salary** (£2,400 in year one, rising over time).
- Over 45 years, with a 5% real return, her estimated total pot value at 68 is £600,000–£800,000.
- Annual retirement income (4% withdrawal): £24,000–£32,000 per year.

Scenario 2: If Emily starts her workplace pension at 33:
- She contributes **8% of salary** but starts **11 years later**, missing out on compound growth.
- Over 34 years, with a 5% real return, her estimated total pot value at 68 is £350,000–£500,000.

- Annual retirement income (4% withdrawal): £14,000–£20,000 per year.

Scenario 3: If Emily starts her workplace pension at 44:
- Over 23 years, with a 5% real return, her estimated total pot value at 68 is £200,000–£300,000.
- Annual retirement income (4% withdrawal): £8,000–£12,000 per year.

After seeing the numbers, Emily decided not to opt out of her workplace pension. Although retirement felt like such a distant thing, breaking it all down helped her understand the value of starting early. The difference between starting at 22 versus at 33 could mean having upwards of £10,000 less per year in retirement.

Emily's pension pot

How much do I actually need for retirement?

When you retire, you won't be earning money. But you'll still have the same basic wants and needs to pay for – food, bills, a secure place to live, and a safety net for unexpected costs. Those unexpected costs will change as you age, and can even turn into things that are more stressful and difficult to plan for, like illnesses. In chapter 9, we talked about how a third of people are likely to rent well into retirement,[5] and planning ahead is especially relevant for renters. The cost of rent can generally increase every 6–12 months, so your pension pot will need to keep up with those increases.

Of course, even if you own your home and have paid off your mortgage, you might still find you're stretched when you retire. Just because you have a house doesn't mean you have spare cash lying around it! But the difference is, as a homeowner you'll have more options. One might be renting out a spare bedroom to bring in extra money. Another might be selling up and downsizing to top up your pension. A third option could be 'equity release', which in simple terms is when you take money out of your property (the 'equity') to top up your savings. So for example, if your home is worth £500,000 and you need some cash, you can ask the bank to 'release' £100,000 of its value for you. But this does mean that if you sell it later on, you'd have to pay the bank back, plus interest, which would reduce the amount you'd receive.

It might be an option for some, but it's not a replacement for a pension. And you should also bear in mind that equity release is a loan secured against your home, which comes with risks. If you're considering it, it's a really good idea to get professional financial advice first. All this is to say: you can have a perfectly happy retirement if you rent, but you won't necessarily have the same security homeowners do, so it's important to factor in your added living costs ahead of time.

Given that most people aren't sure how much they'll spend next week, planning decades ahead can feel impossible. Will you need £20,000 a year? £30,000? Research from the Pensions and Lifetime Savings Association (PLSA) says that, as a single person who doesn't have to pay rent or a mortgage, you'll need at least £43,100 a year to enjoy a comfortable standard of living during retirement (and remember, that's every year over your *whole* retirement). The PLSA says £31,300 a year will give you a moderate standard of living, while £14,400 a year will provide you with a minimum standard of living.[6] If that still sounds a little abstract, let us introduce you to three retirees, with three different retirement funds.

Comfortable • • •

Loves: Pinot Noir

Hates: Her grandson's mullet

♥ ◯ ⧓ • • • ▢

Jean retired on **£45,000** a year.
She has **£830,700** in her pension pot
and **£40,000** in savings.

Retirement age: 65 | Current age: 74

Moderate • • •

Loves: Golf

Hates: Drum and bass

♥ ◯ ⧓ • • • ▢

Omari retired on **£32,000** a year.
He has **£421,760** in his pension pot
and **£32,000** in savings.

Retirement age: 68 | Current age: 82

Minimum • • •

Loves: His allotment

Hates: Snails

♥ ◯ ⧓ • • • ▢

Ronald retired on **£15,000** a year.
He's living off the state pension and tops
it up with **£3,500** from his savings.

Retirement age: 70 | Current age: 80

Minimum

Ronald retired on £15,000 a year. He's living off the state pension (£11,500 per year), and tops it up with £3,500 from his savings.[7]

- **Retirement age:** 70
- **Current age:** 80
- **Loves:** His allotment
- **Hates:** Snails

Meet Ronald. He loves gardening and painting, and spends most of his time pottering around at home. He takes one coach trip to Devon each year and stays in a budget-friendly B&B with some friends.

Ronald has to be very strict with his money. He spends no more than £50 a week on groceries, but this works pretty well for him since he grows so much in his allotment.

Ronald owns his house, which he's lived in for 53 years. His kids flew the nest years ago, so he's in the process of downsizing to add a little extra cash to his retirement pot. He's decided to give up his car and use his free bus pass to get around instead.

Ronald has two grandchildren and spends about £20 on their Christmas and birthday presents.

Ronald has never been bothered about snazzy or expensive things, and finds joy being outside in nature.

He gets by day to day but has to keep a close eye on his money, and worries a little about unexpected expenses that could catch him out.

Moderate

Omari retired on £32,000 a year. He has £421,760 in his pension pot and £32,000 in savings.[8]

- **Retirement age:** 68
- **Current age:** 82
- **Loves:** Golf
- **Hates:** Drum & bass

Meet Omari. He lives in south London but most of his family are based in the US, so he spends two weeks each year visiting them in Florida. He also goes on a yearly golfing trip to Surrey.

Omari loves spending a leisurely Sunday in the kitchen cooking up a feast while listening to Gold FM (if it came out after 1980, he's not listening to it). He budgets £55 a week to spend on ingredients and replenishing his extensive spice rack. He eats out now and again.

Omari owns his own home and is mortgage-free. Refitting his kitchen is too expensive, so he's having it repainted instead to keep it looking fresh.

He has a car, which he plans to replace in the next

seven years, and gets the odd taxi when he doesn't want to drive.

Omari loves taking his grandkids presents when he visits them in the States. Along with the multiple packs of Percy Pigs they demand, he sets aside around £30 per person for Christmas and birthdays. He wishes he could give them more, but knows he has to be sensible with what he spends his money on.

Comfortable

Jean retired on £45,000 a year. She has £830,700 in her pension pot and £40,000 in savings.[9]

- **Retirement age:** 65
- **Current age:** 74
- **Loves:** Pinot Noir
- **Hates:** Her grandson's mullet

Meet Jean. She's incredibly chic, has an active social life, and cruises around the Ionian islands every summer. She does three staycations a year – the Lake District is next on her bucket list, because she's heard paddleboarding is all the rage.

Jean's not really into cooking. It feels like a lot of effort now that she lives alone, so she orders meal kits and ready meals, which she spends around £70 a week on. She also eats out with her wine club pals every Sunday. When she's not swanning around the high street in her zippy little Mini convertible, she treats herself to taxis home from her wine club meets.

She's paid off her mortgage and has £35,000 set aside for some big improvements, like a brand new bathroom to make her home more accessible.

Jean has a big family and is the kind of grandma who slips a £5 note into her grandkids' hands every time she sees them. She also has a budget of £50 per family member set aside for Christmas and birthdays.

While some retirees get to enjoy a comfortable, worry-free future, others end up struggling. That's why taking action *now* by contributing to your pension will make a world of difference to your future self, because there's no getting away from it – different pension pots unlock very different lifestyles.

It's never too late!

Throughout this chapter we've talked about the importance of starting early. But if you're in your 30s, 40s or beyond and haven't started yet, there's still a way to make it work. It'll mean making some sacrifices now to set yourself up for a more comfortable retirement, but it'll be worth it.

Here's the magic formula: take your age, divide it in half and contribute that percentage for the rest of your employment.

For example: if you're starting at 34, take 17% of your income for the rest of your employment and send it to a pension pot. If you're starting at 40, you'll need to contribute 20% for the rest of your employment, and so on.

If you have a workplace pension, the great thing is your employer will match your contributions up to 3%, and sometimes even more. This means you don't have to contribute the whole amount yourself. Things are tougher if you don't have a workplace pension, since you'll have to make all the contributions yourself.

Of course, the younger you start the more manageable it'll be to balance your income and pension contributions – and the longer you'll give your money to grow. But no matter how late you think you've left it, the important thing is to start.

Types of pension

Pensions are broadly divided into two groups. There's the state pension, which the government pays out, and different types of private pension, which you (and your employer) nurture over the years. Here they are in more detail . . .

- **State pension:** this is a pension the government provides, and the amount depends on how long you've worked and paid taxes for. If you qualify, you can claim it when you turn 'state pension age', which is between 66 and 68, depending on the year you were born. (You can check your exact state pension age on the government website.)

At the moment, the state pension increases every April based on a system known as the 'triple lock'. The increase matches the highest of these three percentages:

- how much living costs have risen by (inflation)
- the average wage increase from May to July of the previous year
- 2.5%.

Let's use the rates from the 2024/2025 tax year to see how much state pension you'd get . . . **even if you'd worked for 35 years with no gaps in employment, you'd only receive £221.20 a week, which is about £11,500 a year.** Based on the research we shared earlier in this chapter, you wouldn't even be meeting PLSA's minimum standard of living with this amount. And if you've worked *less* than 35 years, you'll get even less. Women are particularly at risk here, with 1 in 10 taking a career break to care for their children.[10]

In short, while the state pension is a great starting point, it's the bare minimum. That's why it's important to take advantage of other types of pensions, like . . .

- **Workplace pension:** a type of private pension, and also where things get much more exciting (promise). It's managed by your employer, meaning they decide which pension provider to invest your money through, but you can choose how much to contribute. In previous years, employees had to choose whether to pay into a workplace pension or not. But in 2012, the government introduced a scheme called 'auto-enrolment', so all employers had to automatically enrol eligible workers – that's anyone between 22 and state pension age who usually works in the UK and earns more than £10,000 a year. You can opt out, but that's probably not a good idea if you want to set yourself up for a comfortable retirement. Under this scheme, the minimum contribution to your pension savings is 8% of your 'qualifying earnings'. Your employers must pay at least 3%, and you'll pay the remaining 5%. As of the 2024/2025 tax year, qualifying earnings are between £6,240 and £50,270, but the government reviews this every year. (Heads up: they're a little different in Scotland – check the government website for the latest.) Some employers will even go *above* the 3% and match your contributions. All the more reason to put in more, if you can! At some point, you might decide you want to change your contribution – for example, increasing it by 1% when you get a pay rise. To make changes, you usually need to speak to your employer or access your pension scheme online.

Workplace pensions also benefit from tax relief (we'll get to that in a second). And some employers offer something called 'pension salary sacrifice'. This means your pension contribution is taken from your gross pay (your pay before tax), which reduces the amount of your income that's taxable. The beauty of a workplace pension is that you won't see or feel it leaving your account, but it'll make a world of difference when you retire.

There are restrictions on when you can access the money in a workplace pension, but you *can* get your hands on it around a decade sooner than the state pension, which you can access when you're between 66 and 68. Currently, you can access workplace and private pensions when you're 55, but this is rising to 57 in 2028.

- **Self-invested personal pension (SIPP):** a SIPP is another type of private pension, but this is one you set up yourself. With a SIPP, you decide how much money you put in and when, along with *how* it's invested – this is when you'll make a call about the 'risk and reward' we spoke about in the 'Becoming an investor' chapter. If you're self-employed and comfortable managing your own investments, you might want to think about setting up a SIPP, since you won't have a workplace pension. But they're not just for the self-employed – you can have both a SIPP *and* a workplace pension if you want to. Although SIPPs don't benefit from the matched contributions that workplace pensions offer, you'll still get to enjoy tax relief benefits, because SIPPs are another type of investment wrapper. Like a workplace pension, you can start taking money out when you reach minimum pension age, although it's possible to access it sooner in some cases, like if you have a terminal illness.

- **Junior SIPP:** this is a pension you can set up for your kids. (See, it's never too early to start!) If they're under 18, you can pay in up to £2,880 a year on their behalf and the government will top it up with a 25% bonus, to a maximum of £3,600. (These rules can change, so always check the government website for the latest.) If you kept up this yearly contribution until they turned 18, they could have a pot worth £713,000 by the time they reached 57, based on an annual investment growth rate of 5%. Even if we dial these figures way back and assume you only made one £2,880 contribution, this could still leave your child with £58,000 by the time they're 57. Of course, because of inflation this won't be worth the same amount in 57 years' time, but it could still be a brilliant cushion for their retirement. They'll gain full control of the account when they turn 18, so from that point on, they can decide how the money is invested and make additional contributions if they want to.

Tax relief

Tax is a complicated business and we don't cover it in this book because it's such a chunky topic it needs its *own* book. But one thing we do want to mention is tax and pensions, which come together to create something quite incredible called **tax relief**. Governments will always be tinkering with the tax rules, so check the latest, but for now pensions provide one of the most effective ways to reduce tax and boost contributions, so you should try to make the most of it. If you're paying into a workplace pension through salary sacrifice, you get the tax break automatically – your contribution goes straight into your pension pot before you're taxed and your salary lands in your bank account. If you pay into a private pension, the tax relief you're eligible for and how you get it depends on things like your income. But as an example, if you're a basic rate tax payer paying 20% tax, the government would top up every £80 you put in with £20 to make it £100. There are some limits like the annual allowance, which is the maximum amount you can save into all pension pots in a tax year before you have to pay tax. For most people, it's £60,000 for the 2024/2025 tax year, but it'll be different for some, so visit the government website for the full details.

Government policies can always change, but for now it's one of the best deals going when it comes to saving for retirement. It's like getting an instant return on your money, before your pension pot even has a chance to grow! When you finally take money out of your pension, you can usually take 25% of it completely tax-free. The rest of your pension withdrawals will be counted as taxable income, and you'll have to pay income tax on your pension when you take it out.

Consolidating pensions

If you've paid into a workplace pension at every company you've worked for, you might have a few pots dotted around.

You can keep them separate, but some people move them all into one place, which is called 'consolidating'. This can be a handy way of streamlining your life admin. Data shows that the average millennial will have 15 jobs in their lifetime,[11] meaning they could end up with 15 different pensions. And who wants to remember 15 passwords for 15 pension sites? And people truly do lose track – as many as *3.3 million* pension pots have been lost and forgotten over the years, meaning there's £31.1 billion left unclaimed![12] Just bear in mind that there are several fees associated with pensions and these can differ between providers, so this is worth looking into before deciding whether or not to consolidate.

You can usually consolidate online, by post or by calling up your provider. You might get charged an exit fee and lose certain benefits by moving your money, so check the small print first.

When we talk about paying yourself first in all the chapters leading up to this one, what we really mean is that you're paying your *future self* – especially your retired self. Every time you contribute to your pension (and squirrel away money into savings and investments) you're plumping that cushion that'll support you in old age, meaning you can live how you want and enjoy life when you most deserve it.

The Golden Spoon
0528 Treasury Terrace,
Goldenfields, GF9 2XP, United Kingdom

TAKEAWAYS

ITEM	QTY
Plan for the lifestyle you want	1
Make the most of your workplace pension	1
Start early, or start now	1
Keep an eye on your pension pots	1
TOTAL	4

NICE DAY

TAKEAWAYS

Plan for the lifestyle you want: if you're struggling to engage with retirement planning, think about all the things you'll want to enjoy when you have the luxury of free time. More holidays and travel? A lifetime supply of piña coladas? Or simply comfort and stability in your home? Picture your ideal scenario as motivation.

Make the most of your workplace pension: if you're employed, the easiest way to set up a pension is to join your company's workplace pension scheme. Auto-enrol, enjoy the benefit of employer contributions and tax relief, and then sit back and let it do its thing.

Start early, or start now: when it comes to saving for retirement, the earlier you start the better, thanks to compound returns. But it's never too late. If you haven't got a pension yet, there's no better time to set one up than right now.

Keep an eye on your pension pots: whether you consolidate your pots or keep them separate is a personal choice, but try to check in on them from time to time to see how they're performing.

Chapter 13
Putting it all into practice

Congratulations! You know everything there is to know about compound interest, you've got up close and personal with your bank account, and you have a new-found respect for squirrels. In just a few short pages, you'll set this book down and head out into the real world. That's where things get trickier, because family, work and weather are always getting in the way of stuff we know we *should* be doing. This isn't where we tell you to stay home every Friday night reading the *Financial Times*. Learning about money is a hugely import-ant step, but it's only the start of how you change your relationship with it. Managing money ultimately comes down to a series of big and small day-to-day decisions in real life. And often, you'll need to choose between what you want in the moment and what you want for your future. Figuring out that balance is a skill that can take months or even years to finesse, but it's worth doing. Because unless you follow through on that billion-dollar app idea you keep telling your friends about, you'll have to make some compromises. The financial equivalent of drinking enough water every day, but enjoying a fancy cup of coffee now and again.

That's what this last chapter is all about. We've covered every major element of a person's financial life in this book, but that doesn't mean you have to do it all right away. In fact, you shouldn't. The key to making progress is focus and routine – figuring out what matters to you most, then getting into the habit of working towards those things consistently. This is your chance to put those big juicy goals down in writing, then break them down into manageable chunks. So grab a pen and a glass of water (or a bucket of coffee), then settle in for some serious introspection.

Get clear on your goals

They say Rome wasn't built in a day, good things come to those who wait, and that you start writing in proverbs when you run out of things to say. Getting razor-sharp on what you really want long-term will keep you motivated – and now's a great time to set clear intentions for yourself. What are three money goals you want to work towards in the next six months? There are no right or wrong answers here, but your goals are there to bring you closer to the lifestyle you want for yourself and your loved ones. The truer they are to what you actually want for yourself, the more likely you are to work towards them! And it helps to be specific and realistic. So rather than 'sort out pension', which feels overwhelming and vague, be specific and break it down into a series of tiny tasks that are actually doable.

Getting on top of my pension in six months

Task	Timeline	To dos
Track down old pensions from places you've worked	Week 1 [dates]	• Email my old boss and ask about my pension account number
Create an account in a pensions app to consolidate them	Week 2 [dates]	• Check that I won't lose any benefits or pay extra fees if I consolidate • Research pension consolidation apps • Make sure it can support all the old pensions I have
Review my current contributions	Week 3 [dates]	• Use a pension app to see how much my current contributions could add up to • Maximise my employer's contributions
Can I make more room in my budget for pension contributions?	Weeks 4–8 [dates]	• Spot any potential trade-offs I can make to increase contributions • Trial making the trade-off for a month • If doable, set up direct debit or increase workplace pension contribution accordingly

Make managing money part of your routine

Along with the specific goals you have for yourself, it pays to get into a good routine with some of the basics we've covered. Build them into your busy schedule, so thinking about them starts to feel second nature, like brushing your teeth, or apologising profusely when someone bumps into you.

Making a little bit of effort to pay attention to your money can make a massive difference. We don't just mean keeping an eye on how much you spend, though that's obviously part of it. Really, it means swapping money avoidance for money consciousness over the days, weeks, months and years. That's the real secret to being a 'money person'. Not an in-depth knowledge of different stock exchanges – just slowly building your confidence and capability over time.

If you're the type of person who likes a summary and a table, here's one that lays out some of the routine things you'll have to think about in a schedule. If you're not a schedule person, pick three or four things from the list and prioritise them instead (calendar reminders in your phone app help, too).

Remember when you were in school with exams around the corner and everyone had a revision technique they swore by? There were flashcard kids and highlighter kids, and that one kid who said they'd 'wing it' only to end up with top marks. The point is that everyone has their own way of doing things and you're more likely to stick to something if you find what works for you.

Make managing money part of your routine

Daily (a couple of minutes)	Weekly (15 minutes)	Monthly (on payday)	Yearly	As and when
Check your bank balance (or notifications, if you have them on)	Keep an eye on your spending against your budget	Review your budget and adjust if you need to	Plan ahead – do you have any big expenses coming up like birthdays or holidays you need to add into your budget?	Look into consolidating your pensions if you move jobs
Keep an eye on your daily spend	Pay any bills you have due (direct debits help)	Pay your major monthly expenses – rent, bills, subscriptions	Shop around for the best deals on your bills and insurance policies	Make sure you're paying the right amount of tax, and claiming the right benefits if you're entitled to any
	A single small task that sets you up on the path to a more long-term goal	Pay towards debts, savings and investments	Check in on your financial goals, and celebrate your progress?	Keep learning – read books, blogs, listen to podcasts
	Review your budget and adjust if you need to	Review recurring expenses and cull any you don't need any more	Revisit your budget if things change, like the amount of money you have coming in, or your life priorities	
		Check on your credit score		
		Review your savings and investments accounts. Shop around if you feel you're not getting the best deal		

Thank you! Come again!

Take budgeting – you might choose real-life envelope stuffing because seeing the physical cash leave your hands helps you stick to your budget. You might find a snazzy spreadsheet template on the internet that you can colour code and customise to your heart's content. If you know you'll easily let a budget slip when you're busy, you could automate your payments. Once you find something that suits you, it won't feel like such a slog.

Last of all, you should be really proud of yourself

You work hard for your money, so you should feel proud when you start using it to invest in yourself and your future. Noticing how far you've come will keep the positive emotions flowing and the momentum going, which will give you the confidence and motivation to keep at it. So in between checking your bank balance and making sure you're drinking enough water, remember to stop and celebrate! And if we could give you one final tip, it would be this – invest in one of those massive refillable water bottles. It really does help keep you hydrated.

Acknowledgements

Writing a book by 'Monzo' meant bringing together the knowledge and talents of dozens of people around the company.

Maja Bayyoud and Emily Rogers held the pen. They wrote with empathy and wit, threading together expert knowledge and customer insight, guided by Beatrice Borbon's sharp editorial eye. Coral Garvey's creativity and fresh designs made the trickiest topics feel easy to approach. Natalie Malevsky's insight and unique point of view shaped every page. And Lizze Brockman made it happen, bringing everything and everyone together.

A digital bank, this was our first time entering the unfamiliar world of print. Thank you to Zennor Compton, Jessica Fletcher and the team at Penguin Random House for being our guides, and to Charlie Dinkin for her singular sense of humour.

For their leadership and wisdom, we'd like to thank Sujata Bhatia, TS Anil and AJ Coyne.

We're grateful to our experts and advisers, who were so

dedicated to making difficult financial topics accessible and generously gave hours of their time. Anna Davis, Rebekah Hornsby, Emma Metcalf, Matt Mair, Priyanka Arora, Krishen Vaya, Laurie Evans, Jay Clark, Luke Enock, Kunal Malani, Sally Moran, Harry Boyd, Amy Grieveson, Jessica Taylor, Olivia Roost, Kimberley Boston-Dye, Charlotte Alden, Sara Poole, Mike Andrews, Jason Kooner, Richard Evetts, Stuart Tucker, Chris Wood, Sheona Vincent Kilbride, Rich Bromley, Douglas Robinson, Hayley Morgan, James Schafe, Sayjal Mistry, Sacha Paneda, Arun Desai, Rannie Powell, Buki Sule, Chris Doughty, Orla Hill, Saskia Liebenberg, Clare Ridd, Nic Hailes, Tara Morrison, Beth Grace, Freddie Braun, Ben Lawrence, Tierney Cowap, Kiki Loizou and Rhys Edwards.

To our book club of early readers, your feedback was invaluable. And lastly, thank you to our customers – the understanding we've put into this book comes from ten years of speaking to and learning from you.

Notes

Foreword
1 Fidelity Bloom, 'Fidelity Investments money mindset study', 2022.

Chapter 1: Looking in the money mirror
1 Money and Pensions Service, 'UK children and young people's financial wellbeing survey: financial foundations, June 2023.

Chapter 2: Principles for your money
1 Leadership IQ, 'Are SMART goals dumb?', (no date).
2 Murphy M, 'Neuroscience explains why you need to write down your goals if you actually want to achieve them', Forbes, April 2018.

Chapter 3: Facing your finances
1 Everett L and Didarzadeh L, 'Financial Progress Research 2023', Monzo [internal report], 2023.
2 Doughty, C, 'Facing your feed: Staying on top of your money', Monzo [internal report], August 2024.
3 Ofcom, *Online Nation 2024 Report*, November 2024.
4 GOV.UK, Self Assessment, no date.

Chapter 5: Doing money together
1 Monzo, *Love Report*, 2023.
2 Gladstone JJ, Garbinsky EN and Mogilner C, 'Pooling Finances and Relationship Satisfaction', *Journal of Personality and Social Psychology*, 2022, vol. 123, no. 6, pp. 1293–1314.

3 Child Poverty Action Group, 'The Cost of a Child reports', December 2024.

4 OECD, 'Net childcare costs', no date, retrieved 7 February 2025.

5 Institute for Fiscal Studies, *The careers and time use of mothers and fathers*, March 2021.

6 The Fawcett Society, *Paths to Parenthood: Uplifting new mothers at work*, November 2023.

7 MoneySavingExpert, 'Tax-free childcare', no date.

8 Money and Pensions Service, *Children and young people's financial wellbeing survey 2022*, 2023.

Chapter 6: Borrowing and debt

1 Office for National Statistics, 'How are financial pressures affecting people in Great Britain?', 22 February 2023.

Chapter 7: Strategies for saving

1 Bryce E, 'Do squirrels remember where they buried their nuts?', *Scientific American*, 20 November 2023.

2 Money.co.uk, 'Savings statistics', 16 January 2024.

3 Doughty C, Round-ups usage data [unpublished SQL query], Monzo, 2025.

Chapter 8: Becoming an investor

1 The Investment Association, 'Investors call on government to create culture of investment to boost UK households' financial resilience', 19 September 2024.

2 Finder UK, 'Share trading research', 24 June 2024, retrieved 18 December 2024

3 *Ibid*.

4 City A.M., 'British investors buck trend and pour more money into UK equities', 30 May 2024.

5 Bank of England, 'Official Bank Rate history', no date (between 2001 and 2024 at 3.42%, savings interest rates estimated).

6 Wikipedia, 'Freddo', no date. https://en.wikipedia.org/wiki/Freddo

7 UK consumer price index (a formal way to say 'inflation') averaging 3.2% (Source: Bank of England, 'Inflation calculator', no date.

8 2001 GBP–USD average exchange rate £1 x £1.44, 2024 GBP–USD average exchange rate £1 x $1.28 (Source: OFX, 'Yearly average rates', no date.)

9 Estimates of historic returns are based on investing an initial amount of $144.00 with no further contributions ($0.00 per month) for a duration of 23 years, resulting in an annual rate of return of 8.52%. (Source: S&P 500 Data, 'Stock market returns between 2001 and 2024', no date.)

10 UK consumer price index (a formal way to say 'inflation') averaging 3.2% (Source: Bank of England, 'Inflation calculator', no date.)

11 Bank of England, Database, 'CFMB2HW', no date, retrieved 7 February 2025.

12 Office for National Statistics, 'Consumer Prices Index including owner occupiers' housing costs (CPIH), (Version 54), no date, retrieved 7 February 2025.

13 Yahoo Finance, 'S&P 500 (^GSPC)', no date, retrieved 7 February 2025.

14 University of Portsmouth, 'Why good weather isn't a good thing for stock markets', 5 May 2023.

15 The Investment Association, 'Funds list: Fund sectors', 7 February 2025.

16 Morningstar, 'Active vs. passive investing', 23 September 2024.

17 Edwards J, 'Bitcoin's price history', Investopedia, 23 January 2025.

18 Johnson B, 'Should you have a fun portfolio?', Morningstar UK, 22 February 2022.

Chapter 9: Making the most of home and renting

1 Callaghan, D, 'TikTok to "revolutionise property searches and replace portals"', The Negotiator, 6 February 2024.

2 Spears WMS, 'Can TikTok sell prime properties?', 13 March 2024.

3 Pheby C, 'Global: Who does – and doesn't – want to own a home?', YouGov, 29 June 2021.

4 Financial Times, 'How the Bank of Mum and Dad reshaped the British economy', 30 November 2024.

5 UK Government, 'UK House Price Index for January 2024', GOV.UK, 20 March 2024.

6 Institute for Fiscal Studies, 'Hotel Mum and Dad? Co-residence with parents among those aged 25-34', 11 January 2025.

7 Equity Release Council, 'Locked out: Two in five expect to rent in retirement as confusion clouds options', 20 November 2024.

8 Office for National Statistics, 'Families and households: Latest trends and data', no date, retrieved 14 February 2025.

9 Office for National Statistics, 'Private rent and house prices, UK: August 2024', 14 August 2024.

Chapter 10: Buying a home

1 Shaw V, 'First-time buyers stretching out mortgage terms for longer, bank reports', *The Independent*, 14 March 2024.

2 UK Government, *English Housing Survey 2023–2024*, Chapter 2: Housing costs and affordability, GOV.UK, 28 November 2024.

3 HomeOwners Alliance, 'Almost 2 million aspiring homeowners don't think they'll follow in the footsteps of their parents – the generation gap worsens', 26 February 2024.

4 Mortgageable, 'Do mortgage brokers get better rates?', 15 February 2024.

5 Rightmove, 'Rightmove's data, no date, retrieved 29 January 2024.

6 Home Selling Expert, 'What percentage of house sales fall through?', no date, retrieved 14 February 2025.

Chapter 11: Keeping your money safe

1 Bank of England, 'What is money?', 24 July 2020.

2 Office for National Statistics, 'Crime in England and Wales: Year ending March 2024 [Fraud section], 24 July 2024.

3 UK Finance, *Annual fraud report 2024*, June 2024.

4 Ofcom, 'Scale and impact of online fraud revealed', 16 March 2023.

5 NordPass, 'Top 200 most common passwords', no date, retrieved 29 January 2025.

6 Financial Conduct Authority, *Authorised Push Payment Fraud: enabling a risk-based approach to payment processing*, 9 September 2024.

7 TSB Bank, 'TSB issues urgent consumer warning over purchase scams ahead of busy online shopping period', 7 November 2023.

8 Mangan V, Insights from conversations with investment scam victims [unpublished internal report], Monzo, June 2024.

9 *Ibid.*

Chapter 12: Life after work

1   Deloitte, *The 2022 Gen Z and Millennial survey: A global report*, 2022.

2   Department for Work and Pensions, *Final report: Engaging with pensions at timely moments*, GOV.UK, updated 6 February 2024, retrieved 18 December 2024.

3   AON, 'Pension knowledge gap prevalent across millennials', May 2019.

4   Office for National Statistics, 'Life expectancy calculator', 30 January 2024.

5   Equity Release Council, 'Locked out: Two in five expect to rent in retirement as confusion clouds options', 20 November 2024.

6   Retirement Living Standards, Picture your Future, no date, retrieved 4 February 2025.

7   Assumptions made for calculation: annual withdrawal from savings, £3,500; growth rate, 4%; inflation, 3%; years of withdrawal, 15 years (assumed lives until 95); total savings, £47,220.

8   Assumptions made for calculation: annual withdrawal, £32,000; growth rate, 4%; inflation, 3%; years of withdrawal, 13 (assumed lives until 95).

9   Assumptions made for calculation: Jean retired at 65 and plans to live until 95, she's currently 74 (21 years of retirement); investment growth rate during retirement 4% annually (low/medium risk); average inflation rate is 3%; savings is based on an emergency fund for one year of unexpected medical costs, home repairs, etc.

10 Trades Union Congress, 'Women 7 times more likely than men to be out of work due to caring commitments', 8 March 2023.

11 Fennell A, 'Career change statistics UK', StandOut CV, June 2024.

12 Pensions and Lifetime Savings Association (PLSA), 'Brits missing £31.1bn in unclaimed pension pots', 24 October 2024.

Index

Page references in *italics* indicate images.

On a station platform, with nothing to read,
and a four-hour train journey stretching ahead of him...

That's where the story began for Penguin founder Allen Lane.
With only 'shabby reprints of shoddy novels' on offer,
he resolved to make better books for readers everywhere.

By the time his train pulled into London, the idea was formed.
He would bring the best writing, in stylish and affordable
formats, to everyone. His books would be sold in bookstores,
stationers and tobacconists, for no more than the price
of a ten-pack of cigarettes.

And on every book would be a Penguin, a bird with a certain
'dignified flippancy', and a friendly invitation to anyone who
wished to spend their time reading.

In 1935, the first ten Penguin paperbacks were published.
Just a year later, three million Penguins had made their
way onto our shelves.

Reading was changed forever.

—

A lot has changed since 1935, including Penguin, but in the
most important ways we're still the same. We still believe that
books and reading are for everyone. And we still believe that
whether you're seeking an afternoon's escape, a vigorous debate
or a soothing bedtime story, all possibilities open with a book.

Whoever you are, whatever you're looking for,
you can find it with Penguin.